# Creativity For Entertainers
# Volume One

# Creativity For Entertainers
# Volume One

## The Creative Process

Written and Illustrated by

# Bruce "Charlie" Johnson

**To order additional copies of this book, contact:**
Xlibris Corporation
1-888-795-4274
www.Xlibris.com
Orders@Xlibris.com
26306

# Contents

# Acknowledgements

Althea Gibson said, "No matter what accomplishments you make, somebody helps you."

That is certainly true in my case. I am grateful to the many people who have helped me through their encouragement, friendship, and instruction.

I know that most people do not read the acknowledgement page unless they are hoping to find their name. The names listed below may not mean much to others. However, they are very important to me. I hope that they will demonstrate to you that a truly creative person does not reach their potential on their own. They use what others have to offer them.

When people help me, I try to thank them at that time. The danger of starting a list like this is that you always leave out somebody important that you meant to include. I hope those that I have inadvertently left off will accept my apology and know that I truly do appreciate their contributions.

The most important people for me to thank are Bruce L. and Irene Johnson, my parents, and Carole, my wife. I can truly say that without their support my career and this book would not have been possible.

The following teachers in school played an important role in developing my understanding and use of creativity: Herb Camburn, Helen Currie, Robert Greely, Ken Rugg, Bill Smith, Mrs. Vest, and Thomas Wolfe.

These three men played an important role in inspiring and encouraging my use of variety arts as a teaching tool in church: Pastor Tom Lange, Jim Leach, and Pastor Jim Maines.

I am grateful to the following entertainers for their help, support, inspiration, and friendship: Brenda and Kenny Ahern, Albert Alter, Roly Bain, Norm Barnhart, David Bartlett, Mike Bednarek, Marti Vastbinder Bloes, Mary Pat Booth, Donna Branham, Bonnie Donaldson, Don and Dee Burda, Doc Charles Boas, Betty Cash, Terry DaVolt, Barry and Karen DeChant, Randy Christensen, Rick and Kelley De Lung, Karen and Greg DeSanto, Janice Dorsey, Robin Estes, Bob and Cathy Gibbons, Bill Greene, Gigi Hashimoto, Leslie Homman, Jim Howle, Ralph Huntziner, Jim Kleefeld, Duane and Mary Laflin, Jackie LeClaire, Ann Lieske, Ron London, Larry Lubin, Leslie Manning, Brenda Marshall, Mary Beth Martin, Ruth Matteson, Leon McBryde, Jeff McMullen, Vickie Miller, David Mitchell, Lee Mullally, Randy Munson, Angel Ocasio, Debbie O'Carrol, Cal Olson, Open Sesame (Gigi and Rone), Tammy Parrish, William Pearce, Arthur Pedlar, Dena Piraino, Randy Pryor, Joyce Quisenberry, Karen Reinholt, Marc Renfro, Bill and Jeannie Reynolds, Gabriel Roy, Jim and Beverly Royal, Ed Russel, Trudi Sang, Steve Smith, Richard Snowberg, Jan Starns, Ted "Suds" Sudbrack, Anita Thies, and Kitty Waller.

I am grateful to all of the variety artists who came before me creating the foundation that my career has been built upon and leaving a legacy of ideas for me to adapt.

I am also grateful to all of the authors listed in the bibliography for preserving and sharing the facts and ideas that have been part of my education in being a more creative entertainer.

# Are You Creative?

Before reading the rest of this chapter, answer this multiple-choice question.

> I am . . .
> A. Not very creative.
> B. A little creative.
> C. Very creative.

Roger Von Oech, in *A Whack on the Side of the Head*, describes a study commissioned by a major oil company. Concerned by the lack of creativity in many of their engineers, they hired a team of psychologists to study their employees hoping to find a way to stimulate the least creative. The employees were divided into two groups: creative and less creative. During three months of questioning that included educational background, home life, where they grew up, and favorite color, only one thing was discovered that differentiated the two groups: The creative people thought they were creative, and the less creative people believed they were not creative.

## Self-fulfilling Prophecy

So, however you answered the first question, you are probably right. Why? Because it becomes a self-fulfilling prophecy. That is an idea, which may be true or false, but because you think it is true, you act as if it is true, which makes it become true. A self-fulfilling prophecy is a powerful force that can limit what you accomplish. Here are what others have had to say about it:

- "The words 'I am . . .' are potent words; be careful what you hitch them to. The thing you are claiming has a way of reaching back and claiming you."—A. L. Kitselman
- "They can because they think they can."—Virgil
- "Think you can, think you can't; either way, you'll be right."—Henry Ford
- "To expect defeat is nine-tenths of defeat itself."—Francis Marion Crawford
- "A man who doubts himself is like a man who would enlist in the ranks of his enemies and bear arms against himself. He makes his failures certain by himself being the first person to be convinced of it."—Alexandre Dumas
- "Our minds can shape the way a thing will be because we act according to our expectations."—Federico Fellini

If you think you aren't creative, you act as if you aren't creative, which stifles your creativity, and you become less creative. If you think you are creative, you act accordingly, releasing your creativity.

The nature of creativity is such that the first ideas you have for a problem come slowly and may not be very good. Eventually though better ideas start to pour forth.

When somebody who thinks they are not creative approaches a problem, they evaluate the first ideas right away, decide they aren't any good, and declare that only proves they were right, they aren't creative. They then stop trying. One of my journalism teachers in college used an analogy of a reservoir. We all have a reservoir of ideas. A certain percentage of these are good ideas, and the rest are mediocre or bad ones. When ideas start flowing, if you let your internal critic close the spigot because the first ones are bad, the good ones don't have a chance to come out. The greater the flow of ideas, the more good ones will have a chance to get through. To extend the analogy: If you assume when you turn on the hot water tap that the first gust of cold water means the heater is off, and turn off the tap, the cold water won't clear the pipe so the hot water can come. If you are patient and let the tap run, eventually the hot water will get there. Be patient, and let ideas flow. Eventually the hot ones will come. The process of creativity takes time. People who think they are not creative don't take the time to let the process proceed.

Those who think they are creative allow the process to be completed. This was confirmed in research done at Berkeley by MacKinnon in the 1970s. MacKinnon found that highly creative people took longer to study problems and played with them more.

Jordan Ayan talks about limiting beliefs. These are misconceptions preventing people from being creative. One misconception is that you are either born creative or not creative, so you can't learn to be more creative. Another is that only a certain type of personality can be creative. A third misconception is that only specific types of art or activities are creative, and if you haven't succeeded in them you are not creative. Another is that only very intelligent people can be creative. The reason these beliefs limit your accomplishments is that they convince you in advance that you will fail so you don't even attempt to succeed.

Your beliefs are vital to your creativity. According to Jerry Walsh, "The most important precondition for creativity is to believe in it. If you believe there is a big idea then you are apt to find it. If you do not believe in Santa Claus, you are not going to sit under your chimney on Christmas Eve. If you don't believe in Santa Claus, when he comes in you won't see him."

The truth is that we are all born creative. All young children are very creative. According to one study, 90 percent of the ideas preschool children have are original.

## Perception

If we are naturally creative, why don't we think we are creative? Part of the reason is perception. People think they are not creative because they are unaware of their creativity. They don't look for it or simply don't recognize it.

Many people think they aren't creative because it is so common that they overlook it. They aren't aware of their own creative thoughts. A friend got my wife and I interested in bird watching. The number and variety of birds we suddenly saw on our property amazed us. The birds had been there all along, but we hadn't paid any attention to them. They seemed so common that we overlooked them. We didn't take time to look for them. Once we began looking for them, we could find them. Because our friend has more experience looking for birds, she is able to find them quicker and easier. She knows were they tend to be so she starts by looking there. Also, she is more sensitive to things that indicate a bird's presence.

Sometimes we don't recognize our creative moments because of how we define creativity. We often are stuck thinking in terms of CREATIVE things like composing a song, writing a poem, or painting a portrait. Red Skelton was a very creative entertainer. For example, he created some wonderful pantomime routines. However, he felt creativity meant painting, writing, or music. So, he spent a lot of time and effort to establish himself in one of those fields. He painted, wrote short stories, and composed music. Eventually, he was recognized for his paintings of clowns. If he had never experienced that success, he would have still been considered a very creative person because of what he did as an entertainer. He just didn't feel that way. Just because you are not creative in the same way as other people does not mean you aren't creative.

Red Skelton

There are many ways of being creative. According to Dr. Howard Gardner of Harvard University, there are seven types of intelligence: verbal/linguistic, mathematical/logical, spatial/visual, musical/rhythmic, bodily/kinesthetic,intrapersonal (understanding yourself) and interpersonal (understanding others). Each person possesses different levels of each type of intelligence. It is possible to be creative within each type of intelligence. Somebody who realizes a new insight into what is motivating somebody to do something is just as creative as somebody who writes a poem.

We also tend to think of creativity in terms of big accomplishments. We each perform many small acts of creativity during the day. The problem is we overlook them because they aren't grand enough.

Here are some examples of small acts of creativity. None of them will change the world, but they are still creative.

When we went out to restaurants, Carole and I enjoyed a spring green salad with blue cheese, candied walnuts, and raspberry vinaigrette dressing. We decided to copy that at home. I didn't know how to make the candied walnuts or where they could be purchased. I used Ask Jeeves for the first time to do an Internet search and found the directions. That was a creative solution to the problem because I had never done that type of search before and had to experiment to get the results I wanted. After copying the restaurant salad a few times, I decided mandarin oranges might taste good on it. Adding an ingredient was creative. In the fall, we bought some apples that were particularly good, so Carole diced one and used it on the salad in place of the oranges. Substituting an ingredient was creative.

When we stay in hotels, we bring home the disposable shower caps. Carole uses them to hold back her hair while applying her clown makeup. One day a shower cap in its package was sitting on the kitchen counter when Carole was putting some bowls of food into the refrigerator. She took the shower cap and used it to cover one of the bowls. During the summer, she wanted to put half a juicy watermelon in the refrigerator. She didn't want to get the juice on other things on the shelf so she covered the cut end with a shower cap. Using an object in a new way to solve a problem is being creative.

A store I visit frequently has a parking lot entrance on a busy street. It is hard to make a left turn leaving the store, and turning right means I have to go the long way around. Then one day I drove back by the loading dock and discovered another entrance onto a side street that leads to a traffic signal where it is easy to turn left. Finding a better way to do something, even if it is a route to take while driving, is creative.

There are many definitions of creativity, but one that I like is it is something novel and appropriate. If you do something differently from the way you have done it before, and it is an appropriate response to the situation, it is creative.

It does not matter in what area of your life you discover your creativity. The ability to be creative is transferable from one area of your life to another. The same attitudes and techniques that you use to be creative in your private life can also be used as an entertainer. The examples in this book will be drawn both from experiences as an entertainer and my personal life.

People who watch birds keep journals of the birds they have seen. Start a journal of your creativity. If you add, substitute, or eliminate an ingredient from a recipe, write that down. If you use a common object in a new way, write that down. If you find a new solution to any problem you encounter, no matter how minor it may seem, write that down. If you do a performance, and make a change in one of your routines, write it down. You will be amazed at how many times you are actually creative. This book will help you strengthen your belief in your creative ability.

## Making Comparisons

Another reason for doubting your creativity is comparing yourself to others. You see what others have done, and decide that you could never be that good, so you don't try at all. Writers refer to this as the "Shakespeare Syndrome." Carole and I have had the opportunity to travel and see some of the world's best clowns perform. For a while, Carole found that intimidating. She didn't think she could ever match their skills and ability. She dreaded the thought of appearing on stage. However, when she stopped comparing herself to them, and concentrated on what she loved, hospital and nursing home clowning, she discovered her own skills and ability. She is a great clown in a different way in her own venue. When she is working in a hospital, she is extremely creative.

You don't have to compare yourself to another entertainer. The world doesn't need a copy of them. They have made their contributions to the art. We need your contributions to entertainment. What we need is you, performing from your own unique perspective, sharing yourself with your audience in the venue that is right for you. We need you creating material that is right for you and your audience. We need you doing performances that become memories your audience will cherish.

So how creative are you? That is up to you. What ever you decide will become your reality. What beliefs do you have that prevent you from attempting to be creative? How can you challenge those beliefs? Do you think you are creative? Do you look for creative thoughts? Do you expect them to come? Do you recognize them when you see them? Sometimes the craziest most impractical idea contains a nugget of gold you can utilize. Do you unwrap your ideas and inspect them to see what they contain? Do you play with your ideas to see what they can do? Do you have fun with your ideas?

# How to Use This Book

Have you ever wondered why some entertainers are so good at coming up with routine ideas while others seem to find it so difficult? Part of the answer is that some entertainers work harder at creating routines. However, just working at it is not enough. You also need the knowledge to be able to work effectively. This book will help you learn how you can create your own routines.

This book is the first volume of a three-part course in creativity for entertainers. It is for any variety artist who wants to connect more fully with their audiences, perform material uniquely suited to their personality and abilities, and come closer to reaching their potential as an entertainer.

Volume 1 explores the Creative Process. After reading it you will be able to define creativity, describe the steps of the creative process, and consciously use that process to discover and implement more ideas.

Volume 2 explores Tools and Techniques for Creativity. It will help you develop habits enabling you to be more creative, jump start your thinking when you are having difficulty finding ideas, discover new sources of inspiration, and develop a larger number and greater variety of ideas.

Volume 3 is a series of Creative Routines. They are either routines that I have created or that are part of the public domain. They demonstrate how the Creative Process and Tools and Techniques have been used to create routines. Purchase of these books gives you the right to build the props for your own personal use and to perform the routines. (I am retaining marketing and merchandising rights to the routines.) The routines can serve as a starting place for performing; allowing you to experiment with what types of material is best suited for you. However, the routines are just that a starting place. There are many idea prompts to inspire you to create your own variations that will be even more effective for you. Even if you never perform any of the routines in the volume, it is a good lesson in how to create routines.

## It Takes Work

Trumpeter W. C. Handy said, "Life is something like this trumpet. If you don't put anything in it you don't get anything out. And that's the truth."

The same thing is true of this course. The more effort you put into it, the more benefits you will get from it. Throughout this course, you will find exercises, thought provokers, and idea prompts. I know it is tempting to just skip over those. I do that myself in some books that I read. If you take the time to actually do them you will learn a lot more, plus you will have a large number of potential ideas for your own performances.

However, you may want to read the entire book first to get an overview and then come back to do the exercises that interest you the most. There are a few exercises that need to be completed before you look at the "answer" in order to get the most value from them. I will identify those exercises for you.

Magician Tommy Wonder said, "The only way to learn is by thinking yourself. You have to think, you have to work, and you have to study and experiment. You are the only one who can do that for yourself. Don't believe those people who claim they can teach you. They can't make proper decisions or think for you, simply because they are not you. You must do it for yourself; there is no other way. There are no short cuts to real results."

I encourage you to take notes or keep a journal as you read. Writing down the answers to questions in this course will provide you with lots of potential ideas for your own performance. If you do not record those ideas you will loose them. Make a note about those books I refer to that you want to read yourself. Jot down concepts that inspire or challenge you. Record your thoughts so that you can build upon them.

## The Examples

You will find some examples from my personal life. Creativity is a lifestyle, not just something that you turn on when it is time to go to work. The process that you use to create material for performance is the same process that you use to solve problems in life.

There are also examples from the lives of other creative people. Creativity is a process. The end product will be different for a writer, scientist, businessman, artist, and an entertainer. But the process they use to achieve their goals is the same. The same person may use the process to accomplish different goals. Leonardo da Vinci is known as an outstanding scientist and artist. He was supported by wealthy patrons who paid to have him create artwork for them and to develop devices for them. He was able to attract and maintain patrons because he also an entertainer. He organized pageants and parties for them. He was an accomplished musician and would perform at these events. According to Antonia Valentin, Leonardo da Vinci loved conjuring and was a juggler, performing juggling tricks when he entertained his patrons. He was also known for his sense of humor. His scientific journals also served as a joke file and it is believed that he used these jokes to entertain his patrons.

I have included examples of how other creative entertainers have approached their art. One entertainer that you will find mentioned often is Carole Johnson, my wife, who specializes in Caring Clowning and appears as Pookie in hospitals and nursing homes.

Carole Johnson

There are examples from different variety arts specialties. To get the most from this course, read all the examples, even if there is not an obvious link to your particular specialty. The process of creativity is the same no matter what specialty you apply it to. In volume 1, I use a magic trick as an example of writing fish-related jokes and turning them into a routine. The first time that I used that process to write fish jokes I was helping a friend write a juggling routine she performed with fish.

Second, there is the possibility for crossover of ideas from one specialty to another. A ventriloquist may turn a tennis ball into a puppet. They would do the basic three-ball cascade with three tennis balls and then have a discussion with one of the balls about what it is like to be thrown around. A juggler might learn ventriloquism to add the same routine to their act.

A magician might learn to juggle scarves as a way to show them separate before using them in an effect. I have juggled scarves and then used a magic prop called a Crystal Silk Cylinder to turn the scarves into balls as a transition between two routines. After juggling the balls, I used an illusion called a Bengal Net to turn them back into scarves and then performed a magic trick using them. I have used other magic effects to either produce my juggling props at the start of a routine or to make them vanish at the end.

Ian Thom is a puppeteer, clown, and magician. His puppets perform magic effects. Stan Allen is a magician known for his charming act with a rabbit puppet. He has a card selected and then introduces his rabbit who tries to read the mind of the audience member. Eventually the identity of the chosen card is revealed.

Ventriloquist Ronn Lucas used a magic illusion called a Mirror Box to make it appear he was climbing into a small suitcase to have a consultation with Bronco Billy, his cowboy puppet. Another ventriloquist, Jay Johnson used a magic illusion called a Full Light Séance to levitate the head of Bob, his ventriloquist figure.

## Some Important Terms

I will use "entertainer" when I am talking about a positive
example and "performer" when I am talking about a negative
example.

I will try to credit people when I use them as a positive
example. When I use somebody as a negative example, I
will not reveal their identity. First, by this time they may have
identified the flaw that I saw and found a solution. It would
not be fair to document an earlier mistake. I believe that any
entertainment career is a work in progress. I hope that
performers will strive to continually improve their
performance. I know that I certainly made many mistakes
earlier in my career that I have since corrected. I am making
new mistakes all the time. I am aware of some of them, but
haven't yet found a solution. I know there are other problems
that I have not identified yet. I would hate to be known for
those mistakes.

Second, I've learned to be cautious about making negative
comments about anybody. In the early 1980s, I reviewed ice
shows for a trade publication. One ice show included an
elaborate illusion act. I was not very impressed by the magician.
His costume did not seem to fit the rest of the act. He was
wearing a full-length wizard robe while his assistants were
all dressed in modern clothes. I thought his movements were
very stiff and that he did not do much during the act. His
assistants did everything. One illusion was a transposition,
and the person who reappeared did not look like the person
who had vanished. Everything else about the show was of a
very high quality. I thought it was unusual that they would hire
such a poor magician. I started checking and discovered that
he had fallen and broken his leg the day before. The illusion
act was an important part of the show's plot so it could not be
eliminated. The show got the wizard robe out of wardrobe
storage to hide the cast that covered his leg from ankle to
hip. He was on the ice supervising his assistants as they

performed the illusions themselves for the first time. The person who reappeared in the transposition was a body double for the magician, who normally vanished. They didn't have time to find another person who looked like that to use in the Vanish. If I had published my original opinion of the act I would have unfairly damaged the magician's reputation. He did the best that he could under extremely difficult circumstances. He went "beyond the call of duty" to meet the needs of the show as well as he was able.

## An Important Disclaimer

It has been said that you are not responsible for what you were taught, but you are responsible for what you teach. I have tried to be as responsible as possible for what you will read. I have tried to reconfirm everything. If I had observed something from my own experience, I did research trying to find facts to support my conclusion. If I read something interesting, I tried it out myself to verify it from my own experience. I hope that you will do the same thing with this book. Something is not true just because I wrote it here. Don't accept things just because I have said them. Verify things by testing them. Take what interests you from this book, try it out yourself, and continue to use it if it works for you. If it does not work for you, then find something else that does work better.

In the 1974 commencement speech at Caltech, Richard Feynman expressed one aspect of scientific ethics. He said, "It's a kind of scientific integrity, a principle of scientific thought that corresponds to a kind of utter honesty—a kind of leaning over backwards. For example, if you're doing an experiment, you should report everything that you think might make it invalid—not only what you think is right about it: other causes that could possibly explain your results; and things you thought of that you've eliminated by some other experiment, and how they worked—to make sure the other fellow can tell they have been eliminated.

"Details that could throw doubt on your interpretation must be given, if you know them. You must do the best you can— if you know anything at all wrong, or possibly wrong—to explain it. If you make a theory, for example, and advertise it, or put it out, then you must also put down all the facts that disagree with it, as well as those that agree with it."

That was the type of integrity Feynman was known for, and that he instilled in others. I will try to follow his guidelines in this book. When I suggest a theory about creativity, I will try to provide the arguments for and against it. Then you can decide whether the theory is worth testing yourself.

## This Is Just a Step

I hope that this trilogy will be useful to you. I have tried to make it easy to use as a reference source. After you have read it, and need a jump start for your creativity, I hope that you will return to one of the volumes and use it to prompt ideas. I have tried to make each section self-explanatory so you can access ideas at random after reading it once in sequence.

I also hope that you will continue to explore the creative process by reading other books and trying out additional tools and techniques. I have included an extensive bibliography and suggested reading list. Not every book listed was a direct source for this particular volume, but they all helped me understand the creative process.

> "A creative moment is part of a longer creative process which, in turn is part of a creative life."—Tom Wujec

# What Is Creativity?

## Definition

There is no single consensus on how to define creativity. People who write about it and conduct research into it disagree on what it is. Here are some ideas about the nature of creativity that I will be using throughout this book.

According to the *Creative Spirit*, "The essence of a creative act is one that is both novel and appropriate. An innovation is different from what has been done before—but that's not enough: it can't be just bizarre or eccentric. It must 'work.' To be creative, it must somehow be correct, useful, valuable, meaningful."

"An idea is creative to the degree that it is new and useful," according to Jack Ricchiuto. "In the creative process, we rearrange and redesign what already exists into something of value that has never existed before."

When we think of creativity, we tend to think of generating new ideas. But that is only part of creativity. For an idea to be really creative it must be used. Creativity includes making your ideas a reality.

John Kao defines creativity as "the entire process by which ideas are generated, developed, and transformed into value. It connotes both the art of giving birth to new ideas and the discipline of shaping and developing those ideas to the stage of realized value."

Tom Wujec adds a third ingredient to novelty and value. That is passion. "Passion is what psychologists call internal motivation," said Wujec. "This is the desire to do something for the sheer pleasure of doing it rather than for any prize or compensation. The opposite kind of motivation, external motivation, makes you do something not because you want to, but because you ought to. You seek future reward or to avoid punishment."

Creativity in business is not always motivated by passion. However, the most creative entertainers that I know are very passionate about it. Those who do it professionally consider themselves lucky to be able to earn money doing what they love. There are certainly easier ways to earn a living. Those people I have known that became entertainers primarily to generate income quickly burned out and switched to other business opportunities.

Lee Hausner and Jeremy Schlosberg identified four characteristics of creative individuals. They are the desire to improve things, seeing things from a unique perspective, keeping an open mind to new ideas, and taking action.

I believe creative entertainers are those who are passionate, want to be the best they can be, develop a performance style and material uniquely suited to their talents and abilities, and follow through and use that material to entertain audiences.

## Creativity Is Not Anarchy

People naturally resist change. Some instructors fear creativity opens the door to anarchy, laziness, and lower standards of quality because the creative process includes questioning the established rules, traditions, and assumptions about being an entertainer. The opposite is true. When people break rules experimentally, valid rules are verified. For example, a rule of clown makeup design is that the corners of your painted mouth should not extend wider then the outer corners of your eyes. If you break this rule by extending your painted mouth out and up so the corners are over your cheekbones, you will discover that the skin there doesn't move as you change expressions. A painted mouth that wide doesn't change shape so you are locked into one expression. Since a good makeup design enhances the natural expressiveness of your face enabling you to portray a variety of emotions, you have verified that this rule is valid.

Also, a rule says that you should paint your bottom lip red or black and leave your upper lip white. That is also more expressive because the skin near your nose does not move much as you change expressions.

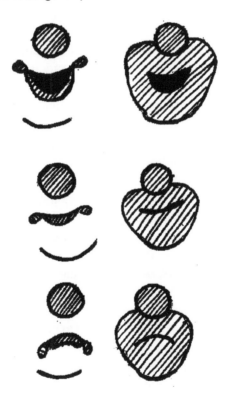

Because creative entertainers discover and understand the basic principles behind the valid rules, they actively support them. As we will see, these individuals create their own personal rules to guide and inspire them. However, they don't try to impose them on others.

"Creative productivity imposes upon the individual a good deal of self-discipline and is most effective with sufficient structure to feel basically secure," said Doris J. Shallcross. "People are more willing to risk if they know their whole foundation won't be obliterated as a possible consequence." Creative entertainers aren't going to tear down the art in search of complete freedom. They know doing that would leave them without any foundations.

## Irresponsibility and Rudeness Are Not Creativity

I know of a group of performers who were thrown out of a supermarket for having shopping cart races up and down the aisles. They had damaged one of the carts, and threatened the safety of other shoppers. They excused their behavior by saying they were exercising their creativity. Next, they went to a restaurant, and were so noisy that other customers complained and then left.

At a clown convention, a half-hour of announcements was scheduled every morning. Although the announcements could have been presented in fifteen minutes, they lasted longer than an hour each day. The person in charge of the meeting kept trying to make jokes, mostly inside jokes the majority in attendance didn't understand. Consequently, expert presenters of valuable information and ideas had to shorten their morning sessions. The person making the announcements wasted valuable time that could have been put to better use, and denied the group of the training they desired.

During a keynote speech at another clown convention, one of the other instructors seated in the audience kept heckling the presenter, attempting to steal attention from him. Afterwards, the heckler's friends gathered around telling him how creative he had been with his jokes.

In each example, the people were not being creative. They were simply being irresponsible and rude.

Creativity does require a free flow of ideas, but that is only half of the process. The other half is evaluating those ideas and implementing the valuable ones. As John Welsh of American Express said, "You ought to be free to have bad ideas, but that is not the same as feeling free to implement a bad idea and therefore to fail."

John Kao calls creativity a balancing act. Among the things you must balance are expressive freedom and self-discipline, personal gratification, and needs of the group, cultural norms and experimentation, and the value of generating ideas and the appropriateness of expressing them.

Children are naturally very creative. As we get older, our creativity is stifled. Many teachers of creativity advocate rediscovering the characteristics of children that makes them so creative. Some clown instructors advocate becoming childlike as part of developing your character.

Everything a child does is not creative. Adults can easily determine if a child is being creative or is merely undisciplined and out of control. Adults can differentiate between creative and destructive behavior in a child. They know if the child's behavior is appropriate. Performers who entertain children know that there is a fine line between playful interaction and disruptive interference, and can recognize when a child in the audience has crossed that line.

A creative person learns to become childlike without being childish. Childlike characteristics include a sense of wonder and discovery, fresh perspective, playful spirit, willingness to experiment and take chances, and a state of constant learning. Childish characteristics include self-centeredness, insistence on being the center of attention, rudeness, inability to delay gratification, and a lack of self-discipline. A truly creative person understands the distinction between childlike and childish, and acts appropriately. They are motivated by the desire to make things better, and refrain from inappropriate behavior that makes them worse.

# Obscurity Is Not Creativity

Some people think being different is being creative, and being different enough is being artistic. They rely on the Emperor's Clothes principle. In the Hans Christian Anderson tale, conmen offer to make the emperor a new set of clothes. They warn him that it will be made out of magic cloth that only the wisest, most intelligent, sophisticated people will be able to see. Wishing everybody else thought they had those qualities, the king and his subjects pretend they can see the nonexistent clothes.

That is what some entertainers literally do. Before a skit competition at a convention, one of the contestants went around telling everybody that "only people with the true heart of the clown will understand my skit." Their skit was meaningless, but I didn't hear many people say that because they didn't want to be accused of not having the heart of the clown.

I've seen this especially in gospel clown ministry. Sometimes the performer will do a skit, usually in silence, with lots of symbolism. It isn't clear what the symbols stand for. The way that they are used may be contradictory. Although the performer is dressed as a clown, they don't do anything humorous. Their message is serious and they don't want to detract from the solemnity surrounding it. The performer may think there is a meaning, but afterwards audience members ask each other, "What was that all about?" Afterwards I have seen other performers flock around them to tell them how creative and artistic they have been. The performer may ask for a critique, but only want to be assured that they are artistic. If you question any of their symbolism they get defensive and inform you that it has great meaning and is clear to those who are supposed to understand. They believe if they don't communicate their message, the Holy Spirit will still reveal it to those who are supposed to receive it.

That is an example of what Tommy Wonder sarcastically calls the "Recipe for Art. Be Vague, Suggest Depth Using Symbolism, and Don't Smile."

Too many performers fall into the trap of trying to be artistic by being obscure. They know that they want to be artists, and this form of abstract performing is the only style they have heard described as artistic. So, they copy what they have seen.

The problem with this approach to art is that you may fool some people, especially yourself, but there will be plenty of people who will see through the charade. In the Hans Christen Anderson tale, a little boy points out that the emperor isn't wearing any clothes. There will always be somebody pointing out that your act is meaningless, and dismissing you as being merely "artsy."

Larry Pisoni, founder of the *Pickle Family Circus*, said, "Ambiguity needs to be avoided at all costs. If anybody in the audience goes 'huh' they aren't paying attention to what you want them to get from the material. Being specific as possible is absolutely required."

A creative entertainer is different, but not too different. John Kao uses jazz as a metaphor for creativity in business. He said, "Even performers of the more conservative forms of jazz search experimentally for the 'sweet spot.' If it sounds too familiar, the music deteriorates to clichés. If it's too obscure, we perceive nothing meaningful from the chaos. Jazz—like business—implies a series of balancing acts. It must always be disciplined—but never driven—by formulas, agendas, sheet music." The same is true about being an entertainer. If your material is too familiar, it is dismissed as being clichéd. If it is too different, it is meaningless.

True art is a form of communication that touches your audience emotionally. One definition of art is "an esthetically pleasing and meaningful arrangement of elements." If your audience is confused about what you are doing, they don't have a chance to be pleased by it because they are trying to figure it out. If they don't know what you are doing, you have failed to communicate with them, and what you have done is meaningless. True art depends upon clarity.

## Creativity Is Not Unique

Being unique is probably an impossible goal. As mentioned by Jack Ricchiuto, "In the creative process, we rearrange and redesign what already exists." There is a limited amount of raw material, and the chances are that we are going to rearrange some of it in a similar way to what has been done by somebody else. Two or more people coming up with the same idea while working independently of each other is called Simultaneous Creativity.

The most famous example of simultaneous creativity occurred on February 14, 1876. On that day, both working independently, Alexander Bell and Elisha Gray applied for patents on the exact same invention for transmitting human speech. Because Bell was the first to arrive at the patent office the patent laws gave him sole rights to the telephone.

Here is an example of simultaneous creativity from my own repertoire. I don't care for one standard version of Multiplying Balls. One ball becomes two. Then one of the balls vanishes again. The performer finds it in their pocket. They add it to the one in their hand so they are holding two. Suddenly they have three. One of them vanishes so they have two again. They take another ball out of their pocket, and put it in their hand so they have three. Now a fourth ball appears, and the trick is over. To me it does not make much sense. The reason for doing it that way is because the performer has to keep adding a ball to their hand before they can do the next multiplication. I came up with a presentation where I start with one ball, which becomes two. I take one of the balls away and put it in a box. Suddenly I have two balls again. I take the extra ball away, put it in my box, and another ball appears in my hand. I devised a method to secretly load a ball into my hand while taking the second ball away. I only pretend to drop it into my box, but retain it in my hand ready to secretly load it into the other hand. I had never seen anybody else do that before, and thought I had come up with something completely original. When I viewed *Tim Wright's Multiplying Ball* video, I was surprised to see that Cardini and many other magicians from the past had done a similar routine. It was so common that it had a name, Perpetual Balls. That does not mean I was any less creative when I developed my routine. It just means that those great entertainers from the past agreed in advance that I had a good idea.

Some performers use simultaneous creativity as an excuse. They say everything that can be created has been, so there is no sense in even trying. If being unique is the only goal of creativity, it is a hopeless goal so there is no need to be creative. That is a misconception. We will see that there are many benefits of being creative that do not depend upon uniqueness.

Some performers become obsessed with trying to be different just to be different. That lets what others have already done limit what you can do. Others control you. An idea may be perfect for you and your audience, but because it has been used before, you dismiss it. Instead of discovering more possibilities as you learn more about entertainment, your potential material is constantly shrinking. Instead of looking for inspiration, you look for constraints.

Trying to be different from others or better than they are keeps you focused on what they are doing. According to Jack Ricchiuto, "In competition, we try to beat apples with better apples rather than with oranges, a fruit drink or innovative fruit product no one has ever tasted before."

Trying to be different can lead to a type of reverse imitation. When Harold Lloyd began working in movies, the top film comedian was Charlie Chaplin. Chaplin was widely imitated. Lloyd's Willy Work and Lonesome Luke movie characters were an imitation of Chaplin's Tramp. His films had plots derived from Chaplin's movies. Lloyd performed gags similar to Chaplin's. In describing the creation of his Lonesome Luke character, Harold Lloyd said, "My father had found a worn pair of Number 12AA shoes in a repair shop . . . In a haberdashery Dad found a black-and-white verticaxl-striped shirt and bought out the stock. The coat of a woman's' tailored suit, a pair of very tight and short trousers, a vest too short, a cut-down collar, a cut-down hat and two dots of a mustache completed the original version of Lonesome Luke. The cunning thought behind all this, you will observe, was to reverse the Chaplin outfit. All his clothes were too large, mine all too small. My shoes were funny, but different; my mustache funny, but different. Nevertheless, the idea was purely imitative and was recognized as such by audiences, although I painstakingly avoided copying the well-known Chaplin mannerisms."

Lloyd met with some box office success, but not compared to Chaplin's. He was not as good as Chaplin at doing material suited for Chaplin. When Lloyd stopped imitating Chaplin, created his own unique "glasses" character, and developed his own "daredevil comedy" style of performance, his career skyrocketed until in some years he passed Chaplin in box office returns and critical acceptance. Harold Lloyd's glasses character was uniquely suited to his personality and talents. Today Lloyd, Chaplin, and Buster Keaton are remembered as the three kings of silent comedy and fans debate which one was the best. (They were each best at what they did.) If Lloyd had continued imitating Chaplin he would be largely forgotten now. Few people remember Billy Ritchie, Billy West, and Charles Amador, who imitated Chaplin during their entire film career.

Harold Lloyd

What you create does not have to be unique. If it is a new idea for you and works, it is creative. It does not matter if other people have also been creative in a similar way.

## Creativity Is a Dichotomy

Being creative often requires balancing two opposite concepts. For example, as we will see it requires both working as hard as possible to consciously generate ideas and not working at all while your subconscious makes connections between ideas. There are two sides to many of the techniques that we will explore.

When Richard Feynman was told there are two sides to everything just like there are two sides to a piece of paper, he replied, "There are two sides to that as well, a Mobius Strip has only one side." (A Mobius Strip is a piece of paper that is twisted once and then the ends glued together. If you start drawing on it with a pencil you will see that you can trace a line that covers both sides without lifting your pencil. It literally has only one side.)

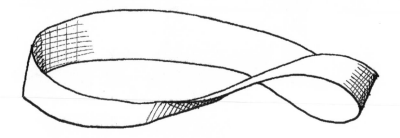

Mobius Strip

## Your Own Definition

Use some dictionaries to look up these words related to creativity: "creativity," "discovery," "ideas," "imagination," "ingenuity," "inspiration," "intuition," "invention," "originality," "plagiarism," "resourcefulness," "revelation," and "vision."

What other words can you think of that are related to creativity?

Get a book of quotations and read what others have said about creativity.

Now write your own definition of creativity.

# Why Should You Be Creative?

If you can't create something truly original, why should you bother trying to be creative?

Because the creative process has several benefits for you specifically and the art of entertainment in general.

## The Joy of Creativity

Being creative is fun. Children are filled with a sense of wonder and discovery that brings them joy. We were having dinner with Will, our grandson, when he was eighteen months old. Carole tasted something and exclaimed, "Mmm, Mmm, Mmm, Mmm, Mmm!" That was a series of sounds Will hadn't heard before, and he laughed. He repeated her, savoring the newness, and then laughed again. They each repeated the sound several more times, and then Will began experimenting with variations, saying it while seated, standing, and sitting in Carole's lap. He kept laughing from the joy of discovery.

Adults have lost that sense of wonder and discovery. We feel we have seen everything before so we stop looking at the world around us. We sense that loss, and wish we could regain that feeling. That is why magic illusions are so popular. A good magician creates a momentary sense of wonder before their audience begins thinking about possible explanations. A great magician is able to prolong that feeling of wonder.

Being creative gives you a license to play. It lets you experience that feeling of wonder and discovery again. There is a sense of wonder in those Eureka moments when you make a new connection between ideas. My good friend Rick De Lung was visiting, and he taught me to vanish a coin using a magic sleight called a Smash Vanish. I think I drove my wife and friends crazy as I spent the next two days enjoying the sense of discovery by smash vanishing all the different possible objects I could think of.

In many of my classes, I use an improvisation exercise called What Is It. There is always a great deal of laughter from participants during that exercise as they experience their creativity.

Experiencing a new idea is not the only source of joy. Performing a new routine for the first time is a time of joy. There is an element of risk. You aren't sure whether the audience will like your new idea. If the audience responds well to it, you feel great joy and wonder. This is reflected in pride and joy in your performance. That pride provides what we refer to as "stage presence."

Joy in performance is vital. George C. Scott said it is one of the three qualities that distinguishes a great entertainer. Joe E. Brown said the audience enjoys seeing us perform what we enjoy doing. The reason Leon McBryde is so loved by audiences is because his great joy during the show is contagious.

Striving to be creative will keep your routines fresh and interesting for you, which will make them interesting for your audience. If you grow tired of your routines, your audience will realize it and won't be interested in them either. By being playful, taking risks, improvising within the framework of your routine, you produce the illusion of "first time." You may have done the basic routines many times, but the audience doesn't know that. To them the show is happening for the very first time. This particular interaction is occurring for the first time, and there is a joy and energy in that.

It doesn't matter if somebody else may have previously created the material you are performing. If it is new to you, and you created it, you receive the emotional boost that provides.

Franklin Delano Roosevelt said, "Happiness lies in the joy of achievement and the thrill of creative effort."

I know that I start to feel grumpy if I go too many days without some creative effort, whether it involves clowning, writing, or solving a problem around the house.

I recently finished painting some customized silk scarves for my show. When Carole saw how hard I was working on them, she asked, "Can't you buy silks like that from somebody?"

No, I couldn't. Nobody sells designs that would work for the routines I had written. That was part of the satisfaction of doing it. The scarves aren't perfect, but I am very pleased that they turned out as well as they did. They weren't easy to do which made the success that more satisfying. When I used the scarves for the first time, and the routines worked, I felt great joy in that achievement.

We each express our creativity in different ways. I do it by creating new clown props or writing. Carole is currently changing the shape of some of our flowerbeds and planning new plantings. She said she does not always enjoy the hard work while she is doing it, but the result gives her great joy. She says it is good for her soul.

Would you like to feel more happiness in your entertainment? How can you be creative? What can you do that is different from what you have done before? What challenges can you set for yourself? What can you attempt to achieve that will give you pride?

## Being Creative Leads to More Creativity

Creative effort increases the ability to be creative. Creativity is like physical strength. It increases with exercise.

Creativity in one area leads to increased creativity in all areas. The creativity I've developed as a clown has often led to creative solutions to problems in my personal life.

People who work to develop original routines tend to also be better at improvisation. By creating new material, you increase your potential for being able to improvise your way out of a problem encountered during a performance. By learning to create, you may be able to discover a solution when it is needed. If all you have learned to do is copy others, you will be left without a solution unless you have seen others encounter the same problem and can copy their solution.

When you are creative, and share ideas with others, they reciprocate. Creative people are attracted to other creative people, and as a group, they become much more creative together. If others know you use ideas to inspire more different ideas, they will eagerly share ideas with you to see what you come up with. When Mary Beth Martin was appearing weekly as a clown on a local children's television show, I had no reservations about sending her my ideas to use. I knew she would approach them creatively. She never copied an idea I sent her exactly, but she changed it to fit her character or used it as an inspiration for another idea. From her point of view, she saw things in my ideas that I had overlooked. When she told me what she had done with my original ideas, I got more ideas back than what I sent her. Some of her ideas inspired still more new ideas I wouldn't have thought of without her impute. That meant I had more ideas to share with her again. Working together, we created many more ideas than we ever would have separately because we inspired new ideas in each other.

To reach your most creative potential you need a flow of ideas to inspire other ideas. When you start recombining aspects from a few ideas you get many more ideas. You won't use every idea you come up with. Some will not be successful. However, they may lead to other ideas that will work.

Here are examples from the career of Walt Disney. He was fascinated by the circus. In 1955, the original *Mickey Mouse Club* TV series premiered, the *Disneyland* TV series debuted, and the Disneyland park opened. Thursdays on the original *Mickey Mouse Club* TV show were circus days. The animated film *Dumbo* was televised as part of the Disneyland TV series that same year. The film was the inspiration for two of the original attractions at the park, the Dumbo Flying Elephant ride, and the Casey Jr. Circus Train. For the first Disneyland

Christmas season, Walt produced the *Mickey Mouse Club Circus* at the park. It featured some of the original Mousketeers performing circus acts. While the rides became enduring favorites, the live circus performance was a flop. Years later, the park had a preview center where they displayed models of coming renovations to the park. One of those was a Circus Land to be built behind Fantasyland. One of the attractions was a sideshow with an Animatronic Goofy performing all the acts. That land was never built. However for two years in a row, 1986-1987, Disneyland and Kenneth Feld Productions co-produced a very successful special event at the park called *Circus Fantasy*. Circus acts performed throughout the park on existing stages. One of the shows featured Deon Aumier performing circus acts while wearing a Goofy costume.

Finally, the area behind Fantasyland at Disneyland was turned into Toontown, inspired by Mickey's Birthdayland, a temporary attraction at Walt Disney World celebrating Mickey's 60th birthday.

## Audience Connection

Creativity allows you to connect with audience members.

In my Chicken Cannon routine I uncover the front of a draped cage revealing a chicken puppet. I take the puppet out and recover the cage. I put the chicken in a cannon. I aim the cannon at the cage, and fire it. I uncover the cage revealing a roasted chicken sitting on the perch.

When I took my chicken puppet out of its cage during one performance, a woman near the front of the audience started laughing. I knew her laughter was loud enough that the rest of the audience could hear it. I immediately covered my chicken's ears as if I was trying to prevent her from knowing she was being laughed at. I looked reproachable at the lady, which only caused her to laugh harder. The rest of the audience joined her as I began petting my chicken, consoling it for being made fun of. By reacting to the woman in the audience, I drew her in. Instead of being an observer of my show, she was a participant.

"Rather than ignoring the audience, react to it if it fits rhythmically into the piece," said Larry Pisoni. "If the audience can hear something, you should too. Play with what is actually happening."

When you display a creative and playful spirit during a performance, you give the audience permission to enter the same spirit. Randy Pryor said, "Our job is to create an atmosphere of play, and invite the audience to join in."

Improvising audience interactions are not the only way to connect with your audience. You can create things in advance. I was hired to entertain at an area meeting for managers of a veterinarian clinic chain. Their office in Issaquah had experienced staff shortages, and people from other offices had helped them by working there on their normal days off. The managers were also discussing other problems the chain was experiencing. They felt that half way through the meeting they would need a humor break to relieve some of the tension. The Issaquah manager arranged for me to carry a doctor bag and distribute "tension relief" pills. I gave everybody one bottle, until I got to that manager. I gave her one bottle, looked at her, and gave her a second bottle. As I continued stacking bottles in front of her, the laughter from the other managers built. The tension was broken.

When performing for a group, I like to use their logo in some way. At the 2001 World Clown Association Convention,

I performed a magic routine using scarves and a paper tube. At the end of the routine, I unrolled the tube to prove that it was empty. Using my computer, I had printed the WCA logo on the inside of the tube. When the audience saw their logo, they sighed and then gave me a nice round of applause. By creating something special for an audience, you are honoring them. They appreciate and respond to that.

What can you do to make a stronger connection to members of your audiences?

## Self-fulfillment

Creativity fulfills our desire for self-expression. We all seem to need to express our personality, to be seen as unique individuals instead of being absorbed into an anonymous crowd. That gives us a feeling of worth. We seem to need to be creative.

Christian illusionist Steve Hart said, "God was the original and ultimate creator. The Bible says we are made in God's image. Therefore, we are made to be creative."

"We are, ourselves, creations. And we, in turn, are meant to continue creativity by being creative ourselves," said Julia Cameron. "The refusal to be creative is self-will and is counter to our true nature."

## Adapting to Change

Allow your act and character to evolve and change. Just because it worked well for you before does not mean it will continue to work as well in the future.

George Burns and Gracie Allen teamed in 1923. They performed a street corner flirtation act titled "Lamb Chops." When they entered the stage, Gracie would notice a man off to the side. When he beckoned to her, she went over and gave him a kiss. Then she returned to center stage with George. When he asked her who the man was, she replied, "I don't know, I've never met him before, and my mother told me not to talk to strangers."

In 1932, Burns and Allen began appearing on the radio, first as regulars on Guy Lombardo's show and then starring in their own series. George said, "Our original format was a variation of the flirtation routine we did in vaudeville. Gracie and I were supposed to be single, and she was being pursued or was pursuing either me or the orchestra leader or the announcer or one of our guests."

Eventually their radio show began slipping in the ratings. George finally realized that their material was too young for them. He told Gracie, "Everybody knows we're married and have the kids, but on the show you're still flirting with everybody. Let's tell them we're married."

With the premier of their 1942 radio season, George and Gracie appeared as a married couple. Their new domestic situation comedy format was written by Paul Henning and Willie Burns, George's brother. According to George, "We were the only couple in the history of radio that got married. And evidently we were funnier married because our ratings immediately began to improve."

Their new format was not only a hit on the radio but was the basis for their classic TV series. After Gracie retired, George tried to continue with the same type of act. He began a new show with the same supporting cast and Gracie being a character that was referred to but unseen. That show was not very popular. After Gracie died, George developed a successful solo nightclub act. Eventually his appearance in *The Sunshine Boys* revitalized his movie career, and he was still performing shortly before his death at the age of one hundred.

George Burns

Sometimes you will be forced by circumstances to change. During six seasons with circuses I had learned how to perform well in that format and had developed many routines suitable for that venue. Then the owner of a circus I was with passed away and her daughter took over the show. The daughter decided she could earn more money during the summer as an act with another show than she could running her own show. She closed down the show for the summer. Suddenly I was out of work. Looking for bookings to fill in, I was hired for the grand opening of a water slide park. They liked what I did, and hired me for the remainder of the summer. I discovered that the requirements of performing in the park were different from circus shows. I had to change some of my circus routines to make them work at the park. Others weren't suitable. I had to create a great deal of new material. When I toured with circuses, I wore traditional tramp wardrobe. The park wanted me to wear something water related, so I created my pirate wardrobe. When I left the park after eleven years, the pirate costume no longer seemed appropriate, and I returned to a more traditional style of tramp clothing.

Many clowns made balloon sculpture a major part of their repertoire. They included it when they visited hospitals. Then hospitals began banning balloons because of patients with latex allergies. That forced hospital clowns to find alternative routines.

Longevity in an entertainment career requires constant creativity. An example is the career of ventriloquist Shari Lewis. According to Jeremy Tarcher, her husband, "Shari had to reinvent herself again and again in order to stay alive in the entertainment business. Repeatedly shifts in the entertainment industry's tastes made it necessary for Shari to find new ways to stay alive."

Shari started off using carved wooden figures. After winning Arthur Godfrey's Talent Scouts in 1953, she was given her own local TV educational program. Three years later a booking on the *Captain Kangaroo Show* was her first appearance on national TV. Bob Keeshan, the show's host and producer, used all soft puppets on his program. He asked Shari if she could perform with a soft puppet. To meet his request, she knitted a lamb puppet that evolved into Lamb Chop. In 1958, she was given her own daily network series. Two years later, the networks moved most of their children's programming to weekends. Three years later, the networks decided to use animated programs that were cheaper to produce and repeat than live programs, and Shari's show was replaced with the Chipmunks. Shari became an author, writing a series of children's books, a syndicated newspaper column for children, and an episode of the original *Star Trek* series. She developed a nightclub act, and regularly appeared as an opening act at the Sahara Hotel in Las Vegas. When rock and country music became the latest fad in Las Vegas, Shari left nightclubs and began appearing on TV in celebrity game shows. When those shows lost their popularity, Shari created special material related to classical music, and began appearing with symphony orchestras. She appeared in a full-scale theatrical production titled *Lamb Chop on Broadway*. Following the growth of the home video market, Shari began her own line of educational tapes. At the end of her career, she returned to TV with *Lamb Chop's Play-Along*, an educational series on PBS.

What things have changed during your entertainment career? How can you adapt to those changes? What new opportunities are open to you?

## Maintaining Growth

As an entertainer, if you fail to develop an attitude of creativity, your attitude creates failure to develop as an entertainer.

According to Tom Wujec, "being creative provides fresh perspectives, novel experiences, and innovative outlooks that helps us grow."

Leon McBryde, an International Clown Hall of Fame inductee, frequently quotes Ray Kroc, McDonald's restaurant founder. Kroc said, "When you are green you grow, when you are ripe you rot."

In nature, things are either in the process of growing or dying. As an entertainer, you can't just sit still. You are either getting better or you are getting worse. Your performances will continue to change. During the summer season at Raging Waters I performed about thirty hours a week spread out over six days. My juggling throws had become so consistent by the end of the summer that I could juggle with my eyes closed because I knew exactly where the ball would land. A few months later with much less performance time, I couldn't do it. Inactivity had allowed my throws to become more varied. You can't prevent changes in your performance. Your only choice is whether the change will be positive or negative. If you aren't working to improve, your skills will deteriorate, and mistakes will become habits.

The way Jan Karon expressed it is, "The firefly only shines when on the wing. So it is with us—when we stop we darken."

According to clown artist Jim Howle, "There are an awful lot of good clowns, and the good ones can get better. It's like they graded us in Art School. We weren't graded on how good we were . . . we were graded on how we learned and progressed. If we didn't progress, it didn't matter how good we were. You just got kicked out of class. You were graded on how much you learn and how much you grow. And that's how I look at clowns. I think that's the test of a clown. The test of a clown and the test of an artist is the test of time."

One of my favorite teachers in college was Herb Camburn. He taught many of my technical theater classes. He gave graduated assignments. For example, in the molding unit of his prop construction class, the item he required you to mold depended upon your previous experience. If you had little design and molding experience, he gave you a simple pattern to copy. If you had some design experience, he asked you to design your own pattern that had to be approved by him. The more experience you had casting molds, the more complicated he expected your design to be. He constantly challenged us to attempt tasks that were more difficult. He also taught us to challenge ourselves. He said if we were motivated only by his expectations, our growth would stop when we finished his classes. If we learned to motivate our own learning, our growth would extend over a lifetime.

There is something called the "zone," "flow," or "white moment." That is a time when you loose self-consciousness and track of time. You feel a sense of harmony, both within yourself and the task at hand. Everything seems effortless. It just seems to click. Your concentration is focused and distractions drop away. It can happen in any field of activity. When it happens to professional athletes, they describe things as moving in slow motion. That moment is the result of your skills being perfectly matched to a challenge. If the task is too easy, you become bored and loose interest. If it is too difficult, you become frustrated and give up. To experience that you must continually challenge yourself to grow as an entertainer. As your skills develop, you have to find new ways to use them. When you accept new challenges, you have to develop the skills to meet them. If you don't find new challenges, you become bored and drop out of entertainment.

Sometimes people ask me if writing or performing gets easier the more that I do it. Not really. As I learn to do it better, my standards of excellence keep changing. As guitarist Pat Metheny said, "Every so often you get it right, and that makes it even more difficult. The standards to which you adhere keeps getting higher and higher."

Here is an example of changing standards. In one of my acts, I produce a punch bowl filled with water from under a piece of fabric. I use the fabric for another effect first. I put it down on top of a square table. When I pick up the cloth, I also pick up a gimmick hidden in the table. The gimmick makes it look like there is a bowl under the cloth although there really isn't one. When the bowl "appears" under the cloth, I carry it over and put it on a round table because the actual bowl was hidden inside that table. I didn't have any other reason for carrying it there. Then I became more concerned with giving my actions a logical motivation. I felt that I needed a reason for not putting the bowl on top of the square table. Eventually, I came up with the idea of producing something else from under the cloth first. Producing an egg made sense within the context of the act. So I began to produce an egg and place it on the square table. Then when the bowl appears I can't put it on the square table because the egg would break. I can't move the egg because I have to hold onto the bowl with both hands to keep it from spilling. So, the only logical choice I have is to put the bowl on the round table. It takes more work to motivate what I do, but I think it results in a stronger performance. (I have since found a different way to obtain the gimmick so I was able to eliminate the square table entirely.)

Even if you could maintain your current level of performance, you would still fall behind. Why? Because performing arts are going to continue to move forward. The history of variety arts is one of evolution and improvement. As Will Rogers said, "Even if you are on the right track, you will get run over if all you do is sit there."

An example is the art of figure skating. When Scott Hamilton won the Olympic Gold Medal in 1984 he performed single triple jumps. Four years later, Kurt Browning became the first person to land a quadruple jump in competition. It takes great skill to do jumps in combination, taking off for the second jump immediately after landing the first. In 1990, Kurt became the first person to do a triple Salchow-triple Toe Loop combination in competition. A year later, he became the first person to land three triple-triple jump combinations during the same performance in competition. In 1997, Elvis Stojko became the first person to land a quadruple-triple combination (both Toe Loops) in competition. By 2002, skaters were performing quadruple-triple-double combinations. In 2001, Kurt Browning stretched the art of skating even further when he created Nyah, a routine without jumps or spins. The routine received standing ovations based on the outstanding use of footwork and choreography.

Perceived limits can be real, until somebody passes them. In track and field, the four-minute mile was considered an impossible barrier. Then once it was broken, many runners achieved it. The sport of joggling is juggling while running. A joggling relay team has even beaten the four-minute mile.

The art of entertainment is going to progress. Somebody is going to make creative contributions that move it forward. You can be that person.

How can you continue to grow as an entertainer? What new challenges will inspire you to improve your skills? What is the next step in your career? How can you begin to take that step?

## Avoiding Being a Commodity

Originally, a commodity was something like gold that could be bought, sold, or traded. One ounce of gold was pretty much like another unless it was turned into a piece of art. Business people have broadened the definition to mean any product or service that is standardized. Sometimes clowns fit into the commodity category, especially those doing birthday parties. In many areas, a clown birthday party is a standardized package consisting of a short magic show (including a Magic Coloring Book and breakaway wand), a couple of games, and balloons or face painting. I know one booking agent that went so far in treating clowning as a commodity that they gave their clowns a list of magic tricks they were required to perform and a list of balloon sculptures they were expected to be able to make. They wanted their clowns to be completely interchangeable so they could commit to a booking without knowing that specific clowns would be available.

A marketing firm that published business directories called to sell me a space in their Seattle book. They had developed a generic business description for a birthday party with a clown. They liked to include clowns in their directory because they didn't have to do any more work, just substitute a new name and phone number on the page that was already laid out. They were surprised when I told them their description didn't fit what I do. They weren't too interested in working with me after that because they knew if they kept going down the list of clowns in the phone book, they would find somebody it would match perfectly.

According to Tom Peters, once your service or business has become a commodity, the only way you can compete is based on price. If all clowns are doing the same act, clients will naturally pick the one that is charging the least. Treating clowning as a commodity is poor business sense, and a disservice to the art of clowning. You should strive to be an individual clown instead of a clone.

When you stand out from the mass of other entertainers, it helps you to gain more bookings. To gain more opportunities to perform you should be able to demonstrate a benefit to using you instead of another entertainer. At one point when most clowns in my area were distributing coloring sheets, I tried to do something better. So, I got small boxes of crayons to hand out with my coloring sheet. When I handed kids a coloring sheet, they might thank me politely. Then when I gave them crayons, they got excited about my gift.

What is it about you that makes you a better choice for meeting your client's needs? How are you different from other performers in your area? The answers to those questions depend upon how creative you are.

## Being True to Yourself

According to Eugene Burger, "The best reason to be creative is to be true to yourself."

Because of your unique personality, interests, and talents, there is something you can do better than anyone else can do it. A couple of clowns took juggling lessons from me frequently during a two-year period. They never learned to juggle because they didn't like it so they never practiced. Most of the clowns they knew personally were also jugglers, so they thought that was what clowns were supposed to do. We attended a performance by Larry Pisoni. One of the first things he did was pull a flute out of his trunk. After some initial comedy about getting his fingers stuck in the ends of the flute, he started to play it. Discordant notes came out of it. Larry starred at the flute a moment, and then turned it around. This time his playing produced a pleasant melody. My friends were shocked. They had both toured professionally as back up musicians, and they had a professional-quality recording studio in their home. They had been so focused on what they thought clowns were supposed to do that they had ignored what they themselves could do. They experienced great success when they began producing clown song and dance acts. Although I can juggle, I have no aptitude for music. I would fail completely if I tried to perform one of their acts. They are much better at what they do than I could ever be.

It has long been accepted that a clown makeup design should be unique and accentuate the natural expressiveness of your face. Clowns realize that copying somebody else's makeup design doesn't work because your face doesn't move in the same way that theirs does. Increasingly clown instructors are teaching that your performing character is really an extension of yourself, accentuating certain aspects of your personality, and that it should be unique. In a similar way, the material you use should be an extension of yourself, accentuating your interests and skills. As Kenny Ahern has said, "use what is unique about yourself as a person to make you unique as a clown."

Marshall Cook's advice for writers is equally valid for entertainers. He said, "Fear makes cowards of us all. We play safe, imitating other writers who are imitating other writers who are imitating other writers. We settle for the trite and true, and when we do, we become less than what we really are.

"You must instead become more of what you are. Discover your strengths and emphasize them. Become more powerful by becoming more authentically yourself when you write. Only then, will you draw fully on the creativity within you and release it in your writing.

"What do you have to offer your reader if not your unique vision, expressed in your unique way? You have yourself to offer, nothing more, nothing less. Offer it all."

When you imitate another entertainer, you are being stingy. You are denying your audience the greatest gift you have to share with them. You are denying them yourself.

According to Larry Pisoni, "When you perform, you expose yourself. The audience gets to know you."

That is what scares people about being creative entertainers. When you create original material, you are revealing yourself. What if the audience doesn't like it? Trust yourself. You are a valuable person that others want to get to know. Trust your audience. They are on your side. Nobody goes to a show hoping to have a terrible time. They want to like you and be entertained by you. According to Peggy Flemming, "If you are honest with your effort, audiences can be very forgiving. In entertainment, people are looking for you to do well."

Be generous with them, share yourself, and they will respond.

*"There's nothing more wonderful than turning a vision into a reality."—M.C. Escher*

# The Problem of Plagiarism

# in Entertainment

People who steal ideas often justify their actions by saying, "In entertainment there is nothing new, everything has been done before." Somebody once excused stealing one of my ideas by telling their club, "This is one of Charlie's routines. I'm sure he won't mind if I steal it, because he probably stole it himself." They were wrong. It was my original creation, and I didn't like them stealing it. I have released many of my routines for use by other entertainers, but that particular routine was a bit that has become one of my trademarks so I reserve it for my own use.

I am not a lawyer, and am not qualified to give legal advice. The following is my opinion based on the information I have been given. For legal advice about a specific situation, consult a qualified lawyer.

## Unethical Behavior

Excusing plagiarism by saying the other person probably stole it first is not new. In 1916, Charles Amador changed his name to Charlie Aplin, copied Chaplin's appearance, and tried to reproduce Chaplin's routines in his own movies. When Chaplin sued him, his defense was that Chaplin's appearance was composed of things Chaplin had copied from others so that it could be copied. His lawyers listed every element of

Chaplin's costume and the name of somebody who had used it previously. For example, George Beban had used the brush mustache in 1890. The Nibble Brothers had used a flexible cane by the turn of the century. The judge ruled that while the elements had been previously used, the "costume en ensemble" had been created by Chaplin, and combined with his name was his exclusive property protected under the law of unfair competition.

Using the same standard for entertainment routines means that although each separate element may have been used before, the combination is a creation belonging to the originator and shouldn't be copied.

## Cheating Yourself

When you copy another entertainer, you are cheating yourself. As long as you are doing material best suited for others, you are not doing the material that is best suited for you.

A copy is always inferior. When you make photocopies of other copies the quality of each succeeding generation is worse. Sharp details become blurred and small blotches become larger. The same is true with entertainment routines.

Subtle touches that made the original version so rich aren't noticed by the imitators and become forgotten. When Dick Van Dyke imitated his friend Stan Laurel on *The Dick Van Dyke Show*, he was careful to get everything just right. When he called Stan to get his reaction, Stan said, "It was just fine Dicky, but . . ." Stan spent the next twenty minutes telling him what he had missed.

Mistakes and flaws in logic are perpetuated when routines are copied. In an open mike show at a *U-W Clown Camp on the Road*® program, Don "Homer" Burda performed a floating table routine. The table was a lightweight one with a nail head sticking up from the center of the top. Don wore a ring that had a slot in it. Slipping the slot around the nail allowed Don to pick up the table, but the appearance was that the table floated and Don's fingers on top were merely keeping it from getting away. The gimmick jammed and Don wasn't able to release the table. He improvised floating movements as he stalled and tried to free the gimmick. Finally, he was able to shake the table loose and catch it with the other hand. Several years later, Don saw a performance by a clown who had been at that show. The clown performed a floating table routine that was a copy of Don's, including some of the moves Don had made trying to release the table. Because this performer's gimmick wasn't jammed, the table didn't stay attached during those moves and suddenly crashed to the ground. He didn't know the purpose for the moves, but thought that since Don had performed them they had to be part of the routine.

Sometimes entertainers who resort to plagiarism aren't smart enough to steal accurately. A dealer at a clown convention in 1990 was selling words cut out of foam rubber. One of the words was "SOMETHING." A creative clown bought that word and used it for a hilarious routine in single skit competition. He held the word in his hands, and said, "I've got something on my hands." He held it behind his back, acted frightened, and said, "I think there is something behind me." He put the word on top of his head, and said, "I've got something on my mind." He screamed, held the word in front of one eye, and exclaimed, "Oh, no, I've got something in my eye!" He continued doing several more similar lines. Although his routine was not a skit technically, he won the competition. Whatever wins tends to be copied. The dealer quickly sold out of the word "SOMETHING" because people wanted to copy the routine. He still had plenty of other words like "TIME," "ANYTHING," and "NOTHING."

Don Burda

The next weekend, I saw a professional performance by a clown who had attended that convention. Since the dealer was out of the foam rubber "SOMETHING," this clown had purchased a piece of foam rubber shaped like the word "TIME." In his show, he held it in his hands, and said, "I've got time on my hands." So far so good. He held it behind his back, acted frightened, and said, "I think there is time behind me." That didn't make complete sense. He put the word on top of his head, and said, "I've got time on my mind." That was possible, but stretching it. He screamed, held the word in front of one eye, and exclaimed, "Oh, no, I've got time in my eye!" People in the audience looked at each other and shrugged. That didn't make any sense. The clown continued using all the lines from the award-winning routine although they were completely inappropriate for the prop he was using. His routine fell completely flat.

Imitation is Limitation. When somebody creates an original routine it capitalizes on their strengths and compensates for their weaknesses. It is limited by their abilities. When you imitate another performer, you are imposing their limitations upon yourself. You are letting what they can not do dictate what you do. Not only are you accepting their weaknesses, you are ignoring your strengths. When you copy somebody else you are also limiting yourself to their thought process and ignoring your own valuable experience, knowledge, point of view, and personality.

Once you've earned a reputation for stealing ideas, you cut off the flow of ideas available to you. I know of one club with several people that steal ideas. As part of their educational program, the club wanted people to perform a portion of their birthday party shows. They had difficulty getting volunteers because everyone knew anything performed would be copied. If people are afraid you will steal their ideas, they become secretive. When you copy ideas, you take without giving anything back. People resent that. They soon exclude you from the flow of ideas.

## Harm to Entertainment as a Creative Art

As a group, clowns tend to condemn people who steal another clown's makeup and costume, but think nothing of people who steal another clown's ideas. Paul Jung said, "The plagiarism of ideas hurts clowning more then copying makeup and costuming."

How does plagiarism hurt entertainment in general?

When ideas can be freely copied, we discourage people from making the effort to create new routines. There is little incentive to try to be unique if everybody is going to immediately copy what you do so you are no longer unique. The art as a whole then stagnates.

Nothing takes the joy out of creation sooner than to hear, "Oh, we just saw somebody else do that." (This happens too often in amateur clown clubs. I've seen it happen in parades, where a clown sees somebody else do a bit they like so they copy it and move ten feet in front of the originator.)

It takes time and effort to create something new. It may also require a financial investment in failed prototypes. The people who work to be creative deserve to benefit from their investment.

When you steal their idea you are also stealing what they invested in developing it.

If entertainers are discouraged from creating new ideas because those ideas will be stolen, we lose more then just the ideas they would have created. We lose the additional ideas that would have been inspired in others. A group of people working together to inspire each other will generate many more ideas then each person working on their own. When stealing makes people reluctant to share ideas, the

source of inspiration for more ideas ends, and everyone
suffers.

## Distinction Between Stealing and Inspiration

Kenny Ahern said, "Be careful of the fine line between
inspiration and imitation."

How do we distinguish between stealing and being inspired
by something? If you change it, improve it, adapt it in some
way, you were inspired by the idea. If you take one element
out of a routine, and use it with elements from other sources
to create a unique combination you were inspired. If you try to
copy an entire routine the way somebody else performed it
you are stealing it.

Perhaps the definition of plagiarism in writing can help
us. The copyright law says that while an idea can be used,
the expression of that idea is the property of the originator.
Also, it allows you to use a portion of another work. There is
a debate on how much you can use, for example, some
people advise that you quote no more then fifty words from
another work. The legal benchmark is whether or not your
use detracts from the originator's ability to benefit from their
creation? The originator has the right to all possible benefits
from the work involved in their creation. To steal from a
written work is stealing from the legal property owned by
another. A piece of writing is legally considered to be an
actual piece of property that is owned, can be sold or rented,
and will be part of an estate passed onto heirs. The copyright
law protects a specific expression of an idea, not the idea
itself.

Translating that into entertainment terms, you can use
the basic idea behind a routine, but the specific way the
routine was performed is the property of the originator. You
can not detract from their ability to benefit from what they
have created.

# Public Domain

To confuse things there is something called "public domain." These items are no longer considered the property of an individual, often because of the length of time that has passed since they were originated. They are owned by the public in general. It is permissible to copy from anything that is in the public domain. You can copy it, but it isn't ethical to claim that you are the originator.

How do you know if something you see performed is an original creation or part of the public domain and available for everyone to use? If it is something you have seen many entertainers perform, it is possibly part of the public domain. It may also be something that is widely plagiarized. The easiest way to be sure is to ask the entertainer you saw use it or consult an entertainment historian.

# Class Room Examples

If an instructor teaches a routine in a class, you can assume they are granting you the rights to perform it. However, if a routine is performed as part of a demonstration show at a convention or workshop, instead of taught in a class, you should consider it like any other show and not copy bits that you see. If somebody performs something in competition, open mike, or a session for critiques, that does not grant you permission to perform it. They are an individual performing in a type of show, not an instructor who has agreed to teach you. Stealing an idea from those shows is just as wrong ethically.

While you can perform routines an instructor has taught in a class, you don't have the right to include it in classes that you teach yourself. That detracts from their ability to earn income by teaching others how to perform it. When you teach, everything in your class should either be public domain, your original creation, or something that you have obtained permission to teach.

## Class Plagiarism

I think one of the biggest detriments to the advancement of clowning is the copycat clown classes and schools. Too many people take the notes from the clown class they attended and use them right away to teach their own clown class. They think that since they "graduated" from a clown class they are qualified to teach one. A party game is to have everybody stand in a circle. You whisper something to the first person who then whispers it to the next. The second person whispers it to the third and so on. It is amazing how distorted the message has become by the time it gets all the way around the circle. The same thing happens with the copycat clown schools. Information gets distorted. As Steve Smith, former Dean of the *Ringling Bros. and Barnum & Bailey Clown College™* said, "We have way too many people believing they're doing something correctly, and they're not. The strength in the current clown organizations and the scores of available conventions is that there is information to be gotten. The problem is that a lot of it is wrong."

A lot of misinformation, particularly about clown history, continues to be circulated. Even after accurate information is made available, the problem persists. The reason for so much false information is that many clown instructors repeat what they have heard in classes without checking to verify if that is correct.

Before somebody begins to teach a class in entertainment they should remember, "You aren't responsible for what you were taught, but you are responsible for what you teach." What you learned in a class should not be taught until you have confirmed it either through your own experience or scholarship.

Copycat instructors not only steal the format and information for the class, they often are also guilty of violating the copyright law by illegally copying and distributing magazine articles.

Reprint rights to magazine articles are valuable. Most variety arts magazines do not pay their contributors. The way that the author is able to make writing the articles financially feasible is to collect them into reprint books or lecture notes for sale. Some of my lecture notes consist of magazine articles combined with new material. I can justify the time and effort spent writing the articles because of the income I realize from selling the lecture notes makes that time profitable. If you wish to continue having worthwhile magazine articles available to read, you need to support the authors by not stealing their property and giving it away free to your classes.

## Conclusion

Entertainers, as a group, should begin considering copying another person's idea what it really is, stealing property that belongs to them. Intellectual property is just as real as physical property. When we justify people stealing ideas we are allowing the art of entertainment in general to stagnate and deteriorate. On the other hand, when we encourage and support creativity we allow the art of entertainment to grow and thrive.

If you are tempted to steal another person's idea, remember that ultimately you are hurting yourself the most.

# Steps in the Creative Process

Some people view creativity as a sudden magical flash of inspiration. They don't know how that happens so they assume it is a "gift" that only some people are fortunate to have. Creativity is actually a process, and anyone can learn to consciously use it on demand.

According to magician George Sands, "Originality or creativity can come about through accident—through a stray overheard conversation—or through a directed goal. The last one (the directed goal) is the most important one. You don't leave it up to accidental happenings or thoughts. You set yourself a problem and then work at it. This is the bread and butter of success. The accidental solution is the gravy. You don't succeed by seeking the gravy. You do succeed by working at bread and butter."

For many people the first step in creativity is stating a question or identifying a problem. For example, a clown skit called Stagecoach is usually performed by two entertainers. I started by asking myself, "Can Stagecoach be performed by one clown?" Then I developed a solo version of the routine.

Here is another example: I was performing a magic illusion called an Appearing Bowl of Water. The standard way to do it includes simulating the appearance of a bowl by draping a cloth over my arm. To me that was a problem because I didn't think it looked like there was a bowl under the cloth. I asked myself, "How can I make it look like there is a bowl under the cloth?" Once I knew what I was looking for, I found a solution. Finding an answer for your question, or a solution to a problem, gives you a goal you can work on reaching.

There are several steps, or roles you play, in reaching your directed goal. Various authors have given them different names, and described them a little differently. Most authors divide the creative process into four steps. It is helpful to look at these different perspectives on the process. It is also important to remember that these are just models simplifying what happens so we can begin to understand it. The human mind is very complex. Nobody understands it completely. The creative process is very fluid. While the steps are described as a sequence, in reality you may go back to earlier steps several times before the process is finally complete.

One of the earliest people to describe the creative process was Graham Wallas. In his 1926 book, *The Art of Thought*, he broke the process down into Preparation, Incubation, Illumination, and Implementation. Preparation is learning everything you can about the project you are working on. In Incubation, you stop working to allow your subconscious mind time to make new associations and work on a solution. Illumination is that moment of insight when your subconscious delivers its solution to your conscious mind. Implementation is the process of putting the idea into action.

In *The Creative Spirit*, Goleman, Kaufman, and Ray change the first step to Immersion. In their version, besides learning everything you can, you push your rational mind to the limit looking for a solution. Then you take time out for your subconscious to work. Because the subconscious works invisibly during the time of Incubation, which separates Immersion from Illumination, outside observers don't understand the work that has been done preparing for the inspiration.

According to Tom Wujec, "These sudden inspirations . . . never happen except after days of voluntary effort which has appeared absolutely fruitless and whence nothing good seems to have come, where the way taken seems totally astray. These efforts have not been as sterile as one thinks; they have set a going the unconscious machine, and without them it would not have moved and would have produced nothing."

Roger von Oech describes two main phases of creativity, the imaginative phase and the practical phase. He said, "The motto of the imaginative phase is: 'Thinking something different.' The motto of the practical phase is: 'Getting something done.'" The imaginative phase is often referred to as divergent thinking. You have a starting point and spread out in different directions to generate as many different ideas as possible. The practical phase is often referred to as convergent thinking. You start with many possible solutions and narrow your options until you decide on the single best one to put into use.

Roger Van Oech, in *A Kick in the Seat of the Pants*, defines the four roles (two in each phase) that you play in the creative process. They are Explorer, Artist, Judge, and Warrior. As the Explorer, you find the raw material that you are going to work with. As the Artist, you combine the raw material in new ways to generate ideas. As the Judge, you evaluate your ideas. As the Warrior, you turn the ideas into realities. His analogy was the first that I learned. It fits the way I think, so it is the one that I will be using most often in this course. It is not the only valid analogy.

Magician Steve Hart refers to the four roles as Adventurer, Wizard, Critic, and Salesman. The Adventurer is a little different than Van Oech's Explorer. It is less goal directed. According to Hart, the Adventurer is on the look out for new ideas by discovering new experiences. As Adventurer, you get out of your daily cycle by meeting new people, take a new class on a subject you have never studied, go shopping, etc. You do things just to have new experiences without knowing how that will be applied to what you are doing. Hart's Wizard and Critic are similar to Van Oech's Artist and Judge. Hart is a business motivational speaker, so his last role is that of Salesman, finding a way to make a profit from your idea.

Magician Tommy Wonder uses building a house as an analogy for creating a routine. His steps are Dream, Technical Details, The Building, and It's Ready—Time of Adjustments. In Dream, you visualize what the final product will be like. You may change your mind several times before it is firmly established. Technical Details means figuring out how to make it a reality. Building is actually constructing it. His final step involves using it and correcting flaws that are revealed.

Sid Parnes and Alex Osborne were two of the pioneers in creativity study. They divided the process into five steps:

1.  Determine the facts.
2.  State the challenge.
3.  Originate a variety of Ideas.
4.  Evaluate the ideas.
5.  Make a plan of action.

No matter what you call the roles, it is important to know when to use them. Each requires a different way of thinking. Applying the wrong type of thinking to the task at hand is counter productive. You also must spend the right amount of time in each role. If you don't explore enough, your artist doesn't have enough to work with. If you spend all your time exploring, nothing else happens.

In actual practice, you will shift back and forth between roles. For example, your Artist may devise a magic routine, but when it comes to implementing it, your Warrior decides you don't know enough to be able to perform it, so you switch back to Explorer to find methods for performing the effect.

Some people get stuck in the preparation phase. I know one clown instructor who started a club for her students to join. In the first two years, her students never performed because they were still working on character development. As long as they were still developing their characters, they didn't have to worry about whether or not an audience would like their character. The preparation stage seems safe. You don't have to find out if you can accomplish anything. It is a way of protecting your dreams. If you try and fail, your dream is over. If you never try, you can continue dreaming about what it would be like to succeed. If you never try to make people laugh, you don't have to consider what will happen if they don't laugh. As long as they are preparing you don't make yourself vulnerable to judgment by others. Preparation is risk free, but you never achieve anything without risk. A baseball analogy is that you can't steal second base with one foot on first.

Another common mistake is to switch too quickly from Artist to Judge. The Judge stifles the Artist and may even kill it. Artistic and critical thinking are mutually exclusive. The best explanation I've seen for why this happens is the Right Brain/ Left Brain model. The Right Mode of thinking is playful and creates new associations. It is the part of your brain that generates new ideas. The Left Mode of thinking is logical and analytical. It is the judgmental part of your brain. When you start to judge your ideas, you shift from Right Mode to Left Mode, ending the flow of new ideas. Any judgment will cause this to happen, even a positive one. Delaying judgment of your ideas for as long as possible allows you to keep working in Right Mode.

Besides the step by step process, Jordan Ayan identifies three other sources for creative ideas, Serendipity, Synchronicity, and Chaos.

## Serendipity

Serendipity is similar to Hart's Adventurer, you discover an idea while looking for something else. Instead of working to solve a problem or create an idea, you recognize an idea when you come across it.

Franklin P. Adams said, "I find that a great part of the information I have was acquired by looking up something and finding something else on the way."

One of my favorite methods of inviting serendipity is to browse through part of an encyclopedia. When I want to look something up, I seldom read only the pertinent article. For example, while using the *Encyclopedia of Magic and Magicians*, by T.A. Waters, to look up a magician who was going to lecture in the Seattle area, I noticed an article on Stacked Decks. That article taught me how to use the Eight Kings method of stacking a deck, which I have used in some performances. Some other encyclopedias that have been particularly useful to me in generating ideas are *Rice's Encyclopedia of Silk Magic* by Harold R. Rice, *Tarbell Course in Magic* by Harlan Tarbell, and *Joe Franklin's Encyclopedia of Comedians* by Joe Franklin.

When I have the chance, I try to take classes from other variety arts instructors, even if I am not sure what I will learn from the class. I often get new ideas that way. Sometimes I can incorporate something that they taught. Often they start me thinking in a new direction and I discover something neither of us would have thought of on our own.

For a variety artist, serendipity can happen anywhere. At a barbershop chorus concert, I heard a song about colors that I think would work well for a magic routine with scarves. I haven't put the routine together yet, but it is in my idea journal for possible future use.

For me, serendipity often occurs in grocery stores. For example, I wanted to make a breakaway spoon. I decided the easiest method was to glue the bowl of a toddler's spoon onto a breakaway wand. At a grocery store, I found a spoon with a handle that was the same diameter as a breakaway wand. I also saw a lunch box container for cookies. It was shaped like an Oreo cookie. I bought it because I knew I would be able to use it for something. At the time, Nabisco was running a popular Oreo's ad campaign with the slogan, "Unlock the Magic." I quickly created a routine where a volunteer picked a card, and I couldn't find the correct one. I invited them to join me in a snack. I brought out the giant

Oreo. I said, "Let's unlock the magic." Unscrewing the container, I revealed a duplicate of their card and some Oreo's. I asked them take a cookie as a thank you for helping me with my act. I didn't notice the card with the cookies, but let them call it to my attention. (I used a method of "forcing" a card to make them select the card I wanted them to.)

Another location I like is a toy store. Brenda Marshall likes to shop for ideas in dollar stores. Wherever you go, don't just look at things as they are, but look at them as potential props or items of inspiration. We refer to this as keeping our "clown eyes on."

Serendipity requires two things. First, you have to go exploring. Don't be so goal oriented that you don't go off on a few tangents. As Henry S. Haskins said, "Don't refuse to go on an occasional wild-goose chase; that is what wild geese are for."

Second, you have to recognize possible ideas when you stumble across them. You need to be open to new thoughts.

## Synchronicity

Psychologist Carl Jung defined Synchronicity as "a meaningful coincidence." You experience something that provides a solution because you are looking for a solution, which makes you receptive to it. It is similar to repeatedly hearing a word that you have just added to your vocabulary. Other people had used the word before, but now you are aware of it so you perceive it.

Part of the explanation of Synchronicity is that we have selective perception. We are bombarded by sensual stimulation. We can't process all of it, so we filter some of it out. I live near a gun range. I'm not aware of the sound of the shooting most of the time. I'm more likely to notice that they aren't shooting. We tune out steady stimulation. That is why you don't constantly turn around to see what is touching your back although your shirt is always touching it.

Without looking up, try to think of five things near you that are red. Now look around you. How many red things do you see? How often have you looked at them without being aware of them? Now that you are looking for red objects, you will see them all around you. We tend to find those things that we are looking for.

You filter out information and ideas that don't seem relevant. Then when you are looking for a solution you turn off your filter and are receptive to the information you need. We tend to remember things that are connected in some way with something that we already know, and to forget other things. Your initial work on the problem makes the information you need relevant so you notice and remember it.

When you ask a question or define a problem, you are allowing synchronicity to begin working.

## Chaos

Chaos theory says, "A very small occurrence can produce unpredictable and sometimes drastic results by triggering a series of increasingly significant events." The most famous chaos proposition is Edward Lorenz's "butterfly effect," which says a butterfly flapping its wings in Hong Kong can start a chain of events that eventually affects the course of a tornado in Texas.

To entertainers this means that you can't always predict what is going to happen in performance. Something small can cause a significant change in a show. Accidents will happen. When the result is beneficial, it is known as a Happy Accident. For example, I perform an old juggling bit where I start letting balls hit the floor. After they bounce, I catch them and continue juggling. I throw each ball a little higher. Finally, I throw one ball very high, and when it hits the floor it doesn't bounce. (It is a beanbag.) I was performing in a high school gymnasium. I threw the beanbag as high as I could, and it didn't come down. It had landed on top of a girder supporting the roof and stayed there. My real shock at what had happened caused a lot of laughter. That was about five years ago. I still sometimes encounter somebody who attended that performance. They always say the ball is still on top of the beam.

As entertainers, we need to move from seeing the unplanned as mistakes and look at them as potential opportunities. Juggler Rhys Thomas says, "Every mistake is a potential new trick."

We can provide chaos room to operate. The Invisible Deck is a gimmicked deck. It allows you to show any card as being the only one reversed in the deck. In the standard routine, you ask somebody to take an Invisible Deck, select one card and remember it, reverse it, and return the deck to you. You then make the deck become visible. You ask them to name the card that they have been thinking of, and show that card is reversed. A member of the Orange County Magic Club added a bit to his presentation. When he produced the deck, he asks the volunteer if they had selected the five of hearts. When they say no, he responds, "That's good, because that is the card everybody picks. Would you tell me what card you did take?" He said he got a tremendous response the one time the volunteer had selected the five of hearts. The volunteer was convinced that he had really read her mind because she hadn't given him any clue to what she was thinking.

In college, I studied scene design and painting. Many of the processes for simulating materials like marble or rocks start in a random manner. You spatter, throw, or dribble paint to create a background texture. Then you look at what has happened, and build upon what is there to create the finished product.

Part of being a creative entertainer is performing enough times that those happy accidents have a chance to occur, and then taking advantage of them. Animation director Chuck Jones said, "The artist in any field must be accident-prone— he or she must stumble, then get up afterward and not walk away, for that is when it all happens. Stumbling is the untoward, unexpected event that corresponds to mutation in genetics. It is the mutation of creativity. Without it we would continue to do only those expected things the experts so adore. Without stumbling, we wouldn't have gotten into the Stone Age—much less out of it. And we would have missed a lot of laughs."

Artist Don Weed has said, "The difference between an amateur and professional is that while happy accidents happen to both, the professional figures out how to make it happen again."

# Left Brain/Right Brain

## The Two Hemispheres

The brain is similar to a yo-yo. It is two halves connected by an axle with a cord leading away from the axle. The cord leading away is the spinal cord carrying messages to the rest of the body. The *Corpus Callosum* is the axle connecting the halves and transmitting messages between the two halves. Each half of the brain is called a hemisphere. In adults, the hemisphere's have different functions.

Here is a metaphor for each hemisphere. The left hemisphere functions like reading a book. It is based on words and works sequentially one page at a time in the proper order. The right hemisphere functions like looking at a painting. It is based on visual images and works randomly seeing the entire picture one moment then zooming in on details in random areas of the painting.

The left hemisphere contains the rational conscious part of your mind. It is analytical and logical. It deals with language, both written and spoken, and math. It counts things and puts them into their proper order. It is involved with our thoughts. It is linear. It makes decisions. The left hemisphere also controls the right side of the body.

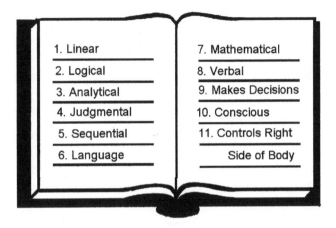

L-Mode Thought

The right hemisphere contains the subconscious part of your mind. It is intuitive and imaginative. It deals with images. It is involved in movement and artistic endeavors such as drawing and music. It stores your memories and recombines them in random order. It is involved in our emotions. It is spatial. It generates new ideas. The right hemisphere also controls the left side of the body.

R-Mode Thought

That is a simplistic description of something that is very complex. According to artist and teacher Betty Edwards, "We have learned that the two hemispheres can work together in a number of ways. Sometimes they cooperate with each half contributing its special abilities and taking on the particular part of the task that is suited to its mode of information processing. At other times, the hemispheres can work singly: with one half 'on,' the other half more or less 'off.' And it seems that the hemispheres may also conflict, one half attempting to do what the other half 'knows' it can do better. Furthermore, it seems that each hemisphere has a way of keeping knowledge from the other hemisphere."

Both Left Brain and Right Brain methods of thought are important in creativity. As mathematician Henry Poincare said, "It is by intuition that we discover and by logic that we prove."

The key is learning when and how to use each type of thought.

## The Location Controversy

Some people have taken a literal interpretation of the terms "left brain" and "right brain." To them, the brain is divided straight down the middle with the two sides having separate and distinctive functions. This has led to some bizarre theories and approaches. For example, what I call the Nostril Theory. It has been observed that people tend to breathe through only one nostril at a time, and they do that in a three-hour cycle. They breathe out of the right nostril for ninety minutes, and then breathe out of the left nostril for ninety minutes. There is one theory of creativity that says you can activate your right hemisphere to generate new ideas by forcing yourself to breathe through the left nostril, which is controlled by the right hemisphere. If you close your right nostril so you are forced to breathe through the left nostril for five minutes, you will continue breathing through the left nostril until the start of the next cycle. According to the theory that activates the right side of the brain so you will generate more new ideas. Several writers claimed that it works, so I tried it. First, five minutes is a long time to hold your right forefinger against the side of your nose. Second, I found that it didn't make any appreciable difference. I suspect that it may be a self-fulfilling prophecy. I was skeptical and didn't expect it to work, so it didn't. It does work for those who think it will. However, if you look at it logically, there isn't any reason for it to work. According to their basic theory, if you use your right hand to press against your right nostril you are activating your left brain, which controls that hand. Wouldn't that larger action with the right hand cancel out the smaller action of breathing through the left nostril? It may be true that breathing through the left nostril involves a portion of the right brain, but that part of the right brain is not necessarily the portion that generates ideas. Also, if their theory is correct, you should be naturally generating fresh ideas in three-hour cycles. I haven't read anybody who makes that claim.

According to Betty Edwards, "While the so-called location controversy continues to engage scientists, the existence in every brain of two fundamentally different cognitive modes is no longer controversial; the corroborating research since Sperry's original work is overwhelming. (See History of the Concept below.) Moreover, even in the midst of the argument about location, most scientists agree that for a majority of individuals, information processed primarily on linear, sequential data is mainly located in the left hemisphere, while global, perceptual data is mainly processed in the right hemisphere.

"Clearly, for educators, the precise location of these modes in the individual brain is not an important issue. What is important is that incoming information can be handled in two fundamentally different ways and that the two modes can apparently work together in a vast array of combinations. Since the late 1970s, I have used the terms "L-mode" and "R-mode" to try to avoid the location controversy."

I will follow Betty's example, and use "L-mode" and "R-mode." I had trouble remembering which side was which until I began using Betty's terms and associating different words with the letters. I think of it as L-mode is Logical while R-mode Recombines ideas and Remembers.

The brain is a complex organ that is not clearly understood. While location remains a controversy, the L-mode and R-mode is a helpful way of thinking and provides useful terms for discussing the creative process. It also has some interesting implications.

## Implications

One thing I've noticed is that the left hand is dominant for some jugglers. Even if they normally use their right hand for other tasks, some people find it easier to do juggling tricks with their left hand. I can only do certain tricks with my left hand. Perhaps the explanation for that is that the right brain, which controls the left hand, is the spatial half. While thinking about the spatial problems caused by the juggling trick, it may be easier to use your left hand. Whether that theory holds true, the result is something to think about. When learning new juggling tricks, try them with your left hand to see what happens. To be the best possible juggler you need to learn to do your tricks with either hand anyway. That allows more possible combinations to be performed.

Some art instructors advocate drawing with your left hand to activate R-mode thinking. According to Betty Edwards, that has limited effectiveness. She said the few people she has observed being able to draw better when switching to their left hand were people who were already ambidextrous or had been left handed early in life and had switched to be right handed. The awkwardness of using the left hand generally off sets the advantage of it being controlled by the right hemisphere. So, Betty's observation of artists contradicts my observation of left-handed jugglers.

Many people have experienced flashes of inspiration during physical activity. The R-mode is involved in physical movement like dance. The R-mode is also involved in new insights. The physical activity activates the R-mode, which then allows you access to the insight. Taking that a step further, doing a physical warm up before a show prepares your muscles to be more flexible, and may switch you into R-mode preparing you to be more mentally flexible. The physical warm up may prepare you for improvisation. I know that I tend to have better audience interactions when I have done a physical warm up before the performance.

You can learn to switch from one mode of thought to another. In *Drawing on the Right Side of the Brain*, Betty Edwards provides several exercises to help you do that.

## History of the Concept

Do you wonder how the right brain/left brain concept began and how it was confirmed?

The two hemispheres and their differing functions were first discovered by observing victims of head injuries. An injury on the right side of the head resulted in difficulties on the left side of the body. An injury on the left side of the head resulted in difficulties on the right side of the body. An injury on the left side of the skull was more likely to affect speech abilities than an equally severe injury on the right. It was concluded that each hemisphere controls the opposite side of the body, and that the left hemisphere controlled vocal functions. The function of the right hemisphere was not understood, so it was assumed it was a less important portion of the brain.

In the 1960s, Phillip Vogel and Joseph Bogen pioneered a radical epilepsy treatment. Some patients were disabled by seizures involving both brain hemispheres. The doctors theorized that the seizures spread from one hemisphere to the other through the Corpus Callosum. They severed the Corpus Callosum in patients who had unsuccessfully tried all other remedies. This did bring relief and the patients regained their health. Both hemispheres of their brain continued to work, but they no longer communicated with each other. These patients became known as *commissurotomy*, or split-brain patients.

At the California Institute of Technology, Roger W. Sperry, with his students Michael Gazzaniga, Jerre Levy, Colwyn Trevarthen, Robert Nebes, and others, began a series of experiments with split-brain patients. For example, one of the things they did was set up a booth that allowed the patient to see one object with their right eye and another with the left eye. If asked to name the object seen, they identified the one seen with the right eye. That verified that the left hemisphere, connected to the right eye, uses words. If they were shown both objects and asked to use their left hand to pick up the object they had seen, they picked up the one seen with the left eye. That verified that the right hemisphere, connected to the left eye, uses visual images. From their experiments, they discovered that the left hemisphere and the right hemisphere work in different ways and handle different types of information. Their continuing research is the foundation for most of the work done in relation to the brain hemispheres and duo modes of thought.

# Explorer

The first role in the creative process is that of the Explorer, looking for material to use in making something new.

## Research Provides Your Artist with Material to Work With

Research provides you with more options to choose from and recombine so that you have a better chance of coming up with the perfect idea.

When I worked at Raging Waters in San Dimas, California, they requested that I wear a costume appropriate to a water theme. I decided to create a pirate costume. A skull and crossed bones Jolly Roger is a stereotype of pirates, but I wasn't sure that was appropriate for a clown. In reading about pirates, I learned that there were many different Jolly Roger designs, ranging from repetitions of skulls to a dead body with a knife in it. Each pirate captain had their own Jolly Roger to distinguish him from the others. I also discovered that when the Jolly Roger flew any enemy that wanted to surrender could join the crew. As the battle raged, the Jolly Roger was taken down and a red flag raised. The red flag was a death sentence for anyone who surrendered or was captured. Learning that a Jolly Roger could be thought of as an offer of friendship made me more comfortable about using it as a pirate clown. The research also made me start thinking about other options for Jolly Roger designs. I decided the skull was important as an identifying trademark. To make it less scary, and funnier, I gave it several missing teeth and one gold tooth. I decided to use crossed swords instead of crossed bones. The swords became a decorative motif I used on other props. I used my customized Jolly Roger on the back of my vest and the brim of my hat. I also used it as a banner on some of my magic tables.

Pirate Costume Design Sketch

Here is another example of the type of exploring I did to create a specialty costume. I designed my own costume for the western themed 1981 *Carson & Barnes Circus* spec. I could have chosen to do a comedy version of an Indian or Cowboy. I selected Cowboy. I went to the public library to consult books on the Old West. I discovered that many cowboys turned up their brims at the front and back instead of the sides. A book on Western films showed me that many of the movie comic sidekicks followed that style of folding their brim. I decided to turn up my brim in the same way. "Tumbleweeds" is one of my favorite comic strips. The title character turns his hat up in the front and back. I copied the scale and proportions of Tumbleweed's hat for my hat. In the old America Sings attraction at Disneyland, a hound dog character sang, "Somebody shot a hole in my Sombrero. Somebody shot a hole in my hat. Somebody shot a hole in my Sombrero. Who would do a terrible thing like that?" So, I made a giant gunshot hole going from side to side in my hat. I learned that there are two styles of chaps, tight fitting, called shotgun, and floppy, called batwing. I discovered in the photos in the western movie book that the hero and villains usually wore shotgun chaps. The comic sidekick usually wore batwing chaps, so I made a pair of batwing chaps for my costume using a pattern from the Tandy Leather Company. Other costume elements were inspired by a picture on a Dairy Queen cup of Dennis the Menace in a western outfit.

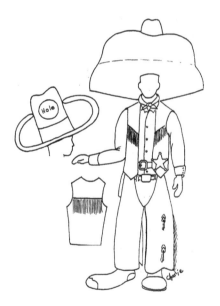

Cowboy Costume Design Sketch

Marshall Cook advised writers, "Creativity seems to thrive best in an environment of abundance or even excess. Gather much more than you'll ever actually use in your writing. That way, you can select from among quotations, descriptions, anecdotes and ideas. The extra material, even though it doesn't appear in the finished writing, will strengthen every paragraph you write."

That is valid for entertainers as well. Everything you learn may not become part of your routine or character. You will know that those things you do select are the best possible ones to use. Also, the additional information makes your created world much fuller and richer. You know it so well that it becomes more real to you. When you believe in it, it becomes more real for your audience. That background of extra knowledge also helps when it comes to adlibbing.

Glen Keane wrote and animated the scene of Cody flying on an eagle's back in Walt Disney's *The Rescuers Down Under*. Keane did a lot of research into the anatomy of an eagle in flight first. He said, "The more I can relate to the eagle and understand the way it moves, the more I can feel like it's me flying in the air. And once I can feel like it's me flying and I'm not just doing a drawing, then it takes the animation to the next level up, and the audience believes it because the artist believes it."

Many entertainers earn extra money by portraying Santa Claus. If you are going to do that be sure to do your research. Santa is supposed to be the expert on toys so you had better become one as well. I was a Santa at a mall in 1990. A couple brought their very young girl up to talk to me. When I asked her what she wanted, she mumbled something. I asked her to speak up because sometimes I get snow in my ears making it hard for Santa to hear. She repeated her request louder but I still couldn't understand it. I glanced at her parents and could tell they did not know what she meant either. I knew that I could not pretend to understand her request so I kept asking her while I struggled to figure out what she meant. Tears of frustration and disappointment welled up in her eyes. Finally I thought she said, "Apple." Thinking quickly I asked, "Do you mean April?" She nodded. I said, "Oh, you want a doll of April the lady reporter who is a friend of the Teenage Mutant Ninja

Turtles." She yelled yes and broke into a smile. Her father said, "Whoa! You're good."

After the little girl had her picture taken, her mother came up and whispered in my ear, "If I believed, you would be the one."

My Santa portrayal was believable because I had taken the time to do my research. The *Teenage Mutant Ninja Turtle* movie had come out earlier that year. I had seen the action figures during my frequent visits to toy stores. That was the only time that I needed to know who April was, but knowing it when I needed it created the perfect moment for that family. Knowing that I was prepared made me a confident Santa. I knew that the real Santa did not know any more about toys then I did.

## Don't Fake It

According to Herb Camburn, "You can't fake it when you are faking it." He meant, when you are simulating or cartooning something you have to know what the real object looks like. You can fake what the object is made out of, but you can't fake your knowledge of it. My prop construction class final project was a crow sitting on the end of a rifle. Herb required that I go back to do additional research into the appearance of crows three times before he approved the final design. That much research paid off. I eventually used the prop in the 1980 *Carson & Barnes Circus* Clown Is King Spec. After one of the circus performances, a veterinarian asked me how long it took me to train my crow to sit on the end of the rifle.

Chuck Jones directed **Bully for Bugs**, a cartoon where Bugs Bunny fights a huge bull. Jones said, "We set about researching bullfighting, not only because it is unwise to work in ignorance, but also because it is a lot more fun to parody something the way it is intended."

Not everyone in the audience will know whether it is right, but somebody will. I wanted to create a painting of a Holy Mackerel for the inside of my trunk lid at Raging Waters. It was a picture of a fish with holes cut through it. I began by researching the appearance of a mackerel, and based my painting on that. One day at the park, I heard a man exclaim, "That really is a mackerel." He knew the difference, and appreciated the fact that I had taken that much effort with my props. It gave me a great feeling of pride to know that was recognized.

Holy Mackerel

There is one person who will always know that it is right. That is you. Knowing that gives you pride in performing your material. That pride is part of stage presence.

## Details

Doing research provides information you can use in creating little details. It is the details that bring something to life. One of my walk arounds is my dog, Frank. Frank is a large hot dog, carved out of foam, placed in an invisible dog leash, a novelty item available from joke shops. When I approached a family, people would smile. The adults would start laughing hilariously when they noticed that Frank had a real dog tag attached to his collar.

According to a book titled *Walt Disney Imagineering*, "Imagineering Senior Vice President John Hench recalls a time prior to the opening of Disneyland when he tried to talk Walt out of wanting to put so much detail on a stagecoach 'Why don't we just leave the leather straps off, Walt?' John questioned. 'The people are never going to appreciate this close-up detail.' Walt turned, firmly planted his finger on John's chest, and replied, 'You're being a poor communicator. People are okay, don't you ever forget that. They will respond to it. They will appreciate it.' Walt had come to know his audience."

The Disney Corporation is an excellent example of research and the use of detail. The Information Research Center at Imagineering has over fifty thousand books and periodicals for use by their theme park designers. They study a subject in depth so they understand the little details that can be incorporated. The next time you are at a Disney park, pay particular attention to their use of detail.

Details do make a difference, even when they aren't consciously perceived. In college, I helped paint a set that included twenty-foot tall marble columns. After the set was assembled on stage, the crew was sitting in the back row of the theater admiring our handiwork. Several of us noticed that the top of one of the columns didn't seem right. We couldn't figure out why. Finally, somebody climbed a ladder to inspect the column closely. They discovered that we had forgotten a pencil line around one of the "blocks" of marble. From the floor, we couldn't see the pencil lines, but they finished the blocks off providing a little separation from each other. Without the line, our minds told us the paint of those two blocks ran together too much without knowing why.

That is why each button on the vest for my tramp clown costume is sewn on with a different color of thread. I have never had anybody comment on it, but it helps create an overall impression of the vest being an old one that Charlie tries to keep in repair.

Adding those little details is part of what Lee Unkrich, co-director of *Monsters, Inc*, calls "sanding the bottom of the drawer—you know, the part of the drawer that you never, ever see. You do it because you're a craftsman and you take pride in your work, and you do it for yourself. It adds to the realism of the world."

Specific details add to the realism. Saying, "he plucked a chrysanthemum," is a lot more meaningful than saying, "he picked a flower."

## Study Entertainment History

Creativity is a cumulative effort. According to magician Eric Lewis, "Nobody creates spontaneously. Everything is based upon, and builds upon, what already exists." When engineers design a new model car, they don't have to invent the wheel all over again. They know a round rolling object is the best way to move the car. They use their knowledge of what has been done in the past, and try to correct faults or make improvements.

Bill Balantine, former RBB&B Clown College Dean, said, "Most great comedy reflects what has gone before: the laughs lie in how the cards are shuffled and how they're played. Every gag has endless variations. The most hackneyed material, altered sufficiently, fitted together expertly, given a flair, can be supremely successful all over again."

Buster Keaton, considered an extremely creative entertainer, incorporated gags others had used before him into his films. He grew up performing on stage in vaudeville and saw a great many other entertainers perform. Some of the gags that he perpetuated and preserved in his films have been traced back to the Hanlon-Lees, the Byrne Brothers, minstrel troupes, and Joseph Grimaldi.

The more cards that you have, the better the chance you will have of coming up with a winning hand. If you have two items, there is only one possible combination, but if you have five items, the number of possible pairs jumps to twenty-one. The more material you have to recombine, the more possible variations you have, the better chance that one of those variations will be successful for you. There is no definitive version of a routine. The history of entertainment reveals that there have been many different variations of every routine.

Learning more about the history of a routine gives you more options to consider. When Greg DeSanto begins working on a new clown act, he researches the history of that routine to get as many ideas as possible. Then he selects those that suit him the best. The result is wonderful routines that get tremendous audience response.

Some of my best routines are based upon old ideas nobody else is currently using. The breakaway racket that I use in my tennis juggling routine is an idea from the February 1947 issue of *Juggler's Bulletin*. In another routine, I ask if the audience would like to see me juggle clubs, and I then juggle three large playing cards of the club suit. That was based on an idea from the September 1948 issue of *Juggler's Bulletin*.

How can you learn more about the history of entertainment? Do something this week to increase your knowledge of entertainment history.

## Other Sources of Information

The Internet has become a wonderful tool for research, but use it cautiously. Anybody can post anything they want without it being screened for accuracy. There is a lot of misinformation spread through the Internet. In looking for information on the yo-yo, I found many Web sites that said it was invented by Philippine hunters who hid in trees and attacked animals by bopping them on the head with a yo-yo. I found just as many sites debunking that theory. There are a lot of sites with false information on the history of clowning as well. Some of them were put up by organizations that you would expect to be accurate.

I've found that children's books are an excellent source of ideas. They give you a feel for what characteristics define a certain role for children. They also condense information down so you can quickly learn the basics without having to read a lot.

Cartoons are another good inspiration source. The bathing suit worn by Goofy in the Disney cartoon *Hawaiian Holiday*

inspired the turn of the century style swimsuit I wore at Raging
Waters.

Swimsuit Costume Sketch

# Basic Skills

Doing research can help inspire ideas. Another part of
being an explorer is learning the basic skills that you need to
realize those ideas. If you dabble in a lot of things, you don't
master anything. At some point, you need to specialize to
become effective.

You can have fun painting without knowing much about
mixing paints. To create masterpieces though you have to
develop a deeper knowledge. You start by learning that you
mix yellow with blue to get green. Eventually you learn to mix
in the shade of blue you are using for the sky to make trees or
hills recede into the distance. The further away you want to
make them look, the more sky color you mix in. You learn that
shadows look more realistic if you darken the color by adding
blue instead of black. You learn that if two objects are close

together, the color of one may be reflected on the other so you mix their colors together as you paint.

It has been said that to a person whose only tool is a hammer, every problem is a nail. Your skills are your tools. The more that you know, the greater the probability is that you will have the right tool when you need it. I know many different ways to produce a silk scarf. In October of 2001, I wanted to produce a string of flags as part of a tribute to the victims of the World Trade Center and Pentagon attacks. I had produced the flags before in other routines, but the methods I had used didn't seem to fit into the tribute. I looked at a list of methods I knew, and discovered one that I don't use often but that was perfect for the new routine. If I knew less about silk magic, I wouldn't have been able to create as effective a tribute. In magic, knowing a lot of potential methods for producing an effect allows you to select the best way to turn an idea into reality.

What can you do to increase your level of skill in your entertainment specialty? What classes are available for you to take? What publications should you be reading? Studying is important, but the only way to really learn is by doing it. What should you be practicing to increase your skill level?

## Go Outside of Your Area

Connect all nine dots with four straight lines. Go through each dot only once. Do not lift your pencil from the paper.

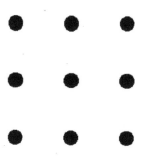

That exercise is the source of the business buzz phrase "going outside the box." To solve it you have to extend the lines beyond the apparent boundaries of the box formed by the dots. (See solution on page 257)

Creativity contains many paradoxes. To be effective, you have to master skills by specializing. If you stick only to your specialty, you block fresh ideas and approaches. You have to be open to things outside your specialty. I don't specialize in balloon sculpture, but occasionally I attend a balloon lecture. I do just a few sculptures that I incorporate into other routines. For example, I balance balloon swords or long stemmed flowers on my chin or nose. I do a levitation routine with a balloon swan. There are many things you can learn from other entertainment specialties and adapt to your needs. In my collection of memorabilia, I have a set of juggling clubs that look like fish. They were used by Kenneth Jones in an Eskimo clown skit. They were made using a process he learned at a puppetry convention.

There are many advantages to learning from other entertainers in other fields, but most entertainers stick close to their specialty. I've observed that performers involved in gospel ministry tend to be the ones who are most narrowly focused on their specialty. Some attend only those educational opportunities that are specifically marketed as being for ministry. Some have an aversion to any program they consider "secular." This is unfortunate because these performers wish to use their skills as teaching tools to share what they consider is important but they fail to develop the basic skill level to become effective communicators. They block off a source of knowledge and ideas that can be very useful to them. Because fresh ideas aren't introduced, existing ideas are copied and perpetuated even if they are ineffective.

In the early 1990s, many clowns performed a skit called Stagecoach. It was performed so often it became a cliché. Why did it suddenly become so popular? It was included in *Bonzo's Complete Book of Skits Volume One*, by Barry

DeChant, published in 1991. Barry is well known among clowns, and his book was very popular. Clowns began performing Stagecoach in skit competition, and others copied it from those performances. So many clowns performed it because they looked in the same place as everybody else and found the same ideas.

If you want to find ideas that are different from everyone else, you need to look in places the others aren't looking. Chandra "Cha Cha" Luce was in a Christian bookstore in the Dallas area. She saw a book written for leaders of church youth groups. The book, compiled by Wayne Rice and Mike Yaconelli, was titled *The Greatest Skits on Earth*. According to the cover it contained 111 "Stunts & Skits" and 78 "Groaners, Quickies, and One-Liners." One of the skits was titled "The Talking Machine." Chandra recognized that it could be performed as a clown skit. She and Brenda Marshall performed it in skit competition at the 1988 Clowns Of America International Convention in Denver. It was their first competition, and partly because it was a skit that the judges weren't familiar with, they won first place.

I've learned a lot about entertainment by watching figurer skaters. I began watching figure skating because I enjoy it, but I soon discovered that I was applying things from it to my own routines. Gradually I became aware that the way the skaters interpreted music, and things said about that interpretation by television commentators, changed the way that I used music in my own performances. My juggling routine using lighted balls in a black out was directly inspired by how figure skaters pair a physical accent to a musical accent. An important lesson I learned was the difference between just doing the choreography and actually listening to the music and feeling it so that it motivated your movements.

Figure skaters work with choreographers. The top skaters tend to work with a small group of the best skating choreographers. The resulting routines tend to be similar. Kurt Browning went outside the art of figure skating to create two of his most famous routines. For his clown routine called Raggidin Time, he worked with a professional clown and with Sandra Bezic, a skating choreographer. For Nyah, a routine without jumps or spins, he worked with a choreographer from the Canadian national ballet. According to Scott Hamilton, Nyah is the masterpiece of Kurt's career.

Look for ideas in areas outside of entertainment. I enjoy movement classes at conferences, and want to improve how I move in my act. My problem was maintaining an exercise program after I returned home. I would be inspired to get started, but quickly become bored. I had bought some movement and physical comedy video tapes produced for clowns, but they didn't help with what I needed. (That doesn't mean the tapes were bad, just that the needs they met were different from those I had.) By looking outside variety arts, I discovered a solution that worked for me, Richard Simmons' *Sweating To The Oldies* video tapes. They are intended as a cardiovascular workout. I found that the dances were many of the exercises I had learned in mime and movement classes choreographed to up tempo songs that are fun. The tapes helped me improve my flexibility and endurance. An added bonus is that I don't have much of a dance background, and the tapes taught me some dance moves I may be able to incorporate into my performances.

British magician Ali Bongo told me that there aren't as many magic lectures in England as there are in America. He said that in England, magicians don't look to other magicians for their inspiration. They find it in other areas. He said his own Shriek of Arabia comedy magic act was inspired by watching a movie about Arabs. He said many of the gestures in his act were copied from Oliver Hardy. He moves at a faster tempo than Oliver does so you don't think of the star of the Laurel and Hardy movies when you watch Ali.

Look for educational opportunities other than those created for entertainers. I wanted to begin making customized silks for some of my magic routines. I discovered a continuing education class in how to hand paint silk in the art department of a local community college.

I didn't learn how to make my tattered tramp clown pants from other clowns. I adapted a method I learned while working on a troll costume for a California State University Long Beach production of *Trudi and The Minstrel.* The costume designer based the troll appearance on the French Fry Goblins in the Ronald McDonald commercials. I doubt that anybody has ever looked at my pants and thought of the Goblins, but that is their inspiration.

Circus Costume circa 1980 Costume Sketch

What knowledge would you like to add to your mix of entertainment? How can you learn about that? What sources outside of entertainment are available to help you do that?

# Be Open to New Experiences

Much can be gained by selecting a topic or a problem, and using that to direct your research. Another aspect of being an Explorer is being open to new experiences, and recognizing the ideas you discover along the way. Business people are often advised to change the route they take to work as a method to generate potential ideas. Seeing something new may inspire a different idea.

You never know where an idea may come from. According to circus legend, a sporting event inspired the classic routine of a car with an enormous capacity for clowns. A clown attending a football game saw the cheerleaders arrive in a single car to start the half time show, and recognized the appeal of the idea. On the other hand, a famous sports idea came from entertainment. Football coach Knute Rochne got the idea for his backfield in motion while watching a burlesque chorus line perform.

The key is recognizing the idea when you see it. Red Skelton's famous drunken impersonation was not based on observing drunks. Watching a toddler's unsteady walk, Red realized that struggle for balance was common to babies and drunks. He studied how the child moved, and used that for his drunken characterizations.

I have a great deal of curiosity. Whenever I go someplace, I read informational signs. When I travel, I like to visit museums. When I attended the 2003 World Clown Association Convention in Jacksonville, Florida, I had an afternoon of free time. I found a tiny historical museum. I did not know what I would find, but I went inside. I discovered that Jacksonville had been an early motion picture center with several studios and was the town where Oliver Hardy began his film career. I learned several fascinating facts about the development of the film industry. I also learned that in the early 1900s Jacksonville had a large neighborhood of African American businessmen who were considered wealthy, but the beaches were all segregated with some beaches reserved for black sunbathers and others reserved for white sunbathers. I learned about the segregation and discrimination that was part of American culture in the early 1900s. It made me further appreciate the accomplishments of Bert Williams who broke through many racial barriers because of his outstanding talent as an entertainer. A tribute to Bert Williams was part of a show I performed the next night at the convention, and I was able to incorporate some of the information that I had learned at the museum.

Seattle has many museums and other educational opportunities. It seems like I don't take the time to visit them until a friend from out of town comes to visit. Then we go to a museum that fits their interests. I wish I would make the effort to go more often on my own.

I recently went on a small ship cruise from Seattle, Washington, to Anchorage, Alaska. During the voyage, I was exposed to many new experiences. One of the onboard activities was a sketching class. After the class, I began sketching a little each day. It was a fascinating way to record my experiences. I rediscovered how much I enjoyed drawing. When I returned home, I took the time to make some new props that required drawing ability.

What museums are near where you live? When was the last time that you visited them? Where else can you go to experience something new?

## Teaching

Many entertainers eventually begin teaching variety arts classes. You are not responsible for what you were taught, but you are responsible for what you teach. Don't just parrot what you learned in classes that you attended. You need to be an Explorer to insure what you teach is accurate. Everything should be verified by personal experience or additional research before you teach it to others.

Other entertainers use their art as a teaching medium. For example, S.M.I.L.E. (Safety Magic In Law Enforcement) is an organization of variety artists who combine safety messages and entertainment. You have to be an Explorer and learn about your subject. You have to be sure that you know what you are talking about. If you want to do drug awareness programs, you have to learn about the drug problem. If your audience knows more about it than you do, they aren't going to give your message much credibility. You need to become the expert in your field.

# Artist

The second role that you play during the creative process is that of being an artist. This is when you will generate new ideas.

## Beginners Mind

There are many stories of amazing breakthroughs made by lucky amateurs because of their fresh perspective. One of the dichotomies of creativity is the Beginners Mind and being an expert. The Beginners Mind is open without preconceived solutions. The expert has the necessary knowledge to make an idea a reality.

While playing the role of artist, you need to find a way to achieve the fresh perspective of the beginner. You need to forget what you know about how it should be done, and explore ways that it might be done.

## Go for Volume

Three of these four objects have something in common. Can you guess what that is and which one does not belong in the group? Apple, Banana, Tomato, and Cherry.

There is more than one possible answer. Tomatoes are an annual dying off at the end of the season, while the other three plants live for many years. Bananas are a sub-tropical fruit and the other three are temperate-zone fruits. Tomatoes are bushy while the other three are considered to grow on trees. Cherries are the only stone fruits (containing a pit) in the group. Tomatoes were considered poisonous in the United States until the nineteenth century, while the other three have been cultivated and consumed for centuries. Bananas are generally yellow when ripe, while the other three have popular red varieties. (There are a few red varieties of bananas, but they aren't very popular.) Cherries are red or purple when ripe, while the other three have varieties that are yellow when ripe. Tomatoes are used in garden salads while the other three are used in fruit salads.

There is often more than one "right" answer in entertainment. There is no single right way to perform a routine. Don't be satisfied with the first right answer you find. Looking for additional right answers opens up your creativity and often leads you to a better solution.

Emile Chartier said, "Nothing is more dangerous than an idea when it's the only one you have."

Don't stop with the obvious answer. Try to go beyond that. Always ask yourself, "what else might work?"

Beware of instructors who tell you their way is the only right way to do something. Entertainment is a creative, personal art. What is best for somebody else may not be best for you.

Scott Adams said, "If you're going to create, create a lot. Creativity is not like playing the slot machines, where failure to win means you go home broke. With creativity, if you don't win, you're usually no worse off than if you hadn't played."

Your goal as an artist is to generate as many different ideas as possible. Quantity leads to quality simply because you have more to select from when looking for the best answer.

John Welsh of American Express said, "You ought to be free to have bad ideas because at least 90 percent of your ideas will be bad if you have enough ideas to have good ideas."

Many creativity writers agree with John Welsh's estimate. That may seem depressing, but it is also liberating. It frees you from the pressure of having to come up with good ideas. You know that the majority of ideas won't be useable so you don't have to worry about it. It also means that if you generate enough ideas, the odds are that they will include useable ideas. If you can come up with ten ideas, one of them should be useable. If you start with a hundred ideas, you will have ten useable ideas to select from when picking the best.

Throughout this book, you will find techniques and idea generators to assist your artist in making new connections that can become useable ideas. Cartoonist Lynn Johnston said, "Like starting an old chainsaw that's hard to start, you often have to try every trick of the trade before work can begin!"

## Timing

Are you a chicken or an owl? We each have biological rhythms. Some people are early risers, get a lot done rapidly, and fade in the afternoon. Others sleep later, seem to take a while to really get rolling, and are still going strong late at night. It doesn't matter which pattern you fit into. The important thing is to take advantage of it.

Everyone has times when they feel they can work most efficiently and are more creative. That may be early morning, late morning, middle of the afternoon, evening, or late at night. Pay attention to your rhythm, and schedule your activities accordingly. I am definitely an owl. So, I do routine tasks earlier in the day and schedule my creative efforts for later after I've really started perking.

Not only do you have a time when you start being the most creative, but there is also a time when your creativity shuts off. Trying to push past that time can lead to decreasing results and increasing frustration. Know when you have accomplished enough and that it is time to stop.

When do you have the most energy? When do ideas seem to flow the easiest? How can you arrange to do your creative work then? What do you need to do at other times to have your peak time available for creativity?

## Environment and Rituals

Lynn Johnston wrote, "There is a small sun room off our bedroom that overlooks a thick stand of birch trees. In this room, I keep a beach chair, an old carved table, some plants, a telephone, and a large wooden flamingo. This is my 'writing place.' It is here that I go to await inspiration!"

Many writers and cartoonists set up a "writing place." The description of each varies. Some need natural sunlight and a feeling of openness. Others need the coziness of a secluded corner of the basement. I know some entertainers who rent space in a dance studio. Others arrange to use the fellowship hall at a church. What they all have in common is a place where they expect to work on ideas. That expectation helps shift into thinking creatively.

Often creative people will fill their workspace with items of inspiration. Monica Woods asks, "What's in your work space? Do you surround yourself with objects that inspire your work, recall magical times, soothe your mood, and buoy your flagging spirits? If not, it's time to take inventory. Make your space compatible with your creative impulses."

On top of my computer desk, I have a figment of my imagination. It is a little statue of Figment, a character from the original Imagination pavilion at Epcot in Orlando, Fl. There is also a small triceratops statue. That is my favorite dinosaur, and someday I am going to create a routine with a triceratops in it. On the walls, I have paintings of Emmett Kelly and Otto Griebling. They are positioned so they appear to be watching me as I work. Around my computer screen, I post favorite cartoons and inspiring Bible verses. The verses I currently have posted are II Peter 1: 5-7 and Psalm 51: 10-12. One of the cartoons is the June 12, 2001, panel of John McPherson's "Close To Home." It depicts M. C. Escher as a child building a sandcastle. It makes me smile to see it, and I hope that one of these days I will be able to incorporate an Escher style optical illusion into one of my routines. Another comic strip reminds me of how I want to treat people. It is the May 24, 2001, "Drabble" cartoon by Kevin Fagan. Drabble's father, looking at all the notes and pictures posted on the outside of a refrigerator, thinks, "what a mess! Oh, well. Refrigerators are a lot like people. What's on the inside is more important than what's on the outside."

In addition, I try to make my work area as efficient as possible. Without getting out of my chair, I can reach my phone, computer keyboard, scanner, printer, a supply of paper, pens, pencils, and other office supplies. I have a wall calendar so when somebody calls about a booking, I can turn and see with a glance whether that date is available. When I am working on a writing project, the relevant research resources are usually stacked around me. In the midst of a project, my desk looks like a mess, but I know which pile everything is in and can quickly find it. Other people can't work that way at all. They find any kind of clutter distracting. They have to have things neatly arranged in file folders. You need to find a method that works best for you.

Besides having a space conducive to being creative, many people have rituals for preparing to work. Some writers don't begin until they sharpen all of their pencils. One of my costume teachers in college always began working on a design by putting on a sweatshirt from the university she had attended. Some people can't start work until they have had their second cup of coffee. All of these rituals are a form of conditioned response. They were something the person did in the past when they were creative, so doing them now signals their brain that they desire to be creative.

Where do you feel comfortable working on new material? What type of environment feels creative to you? Is there someplace you reserve for being creative? What type of workspace can you create? What can you do to make it easier for you to work there? What kinds of things do you find inspiring? How can you incorporate them into your workspace? What kinds of things do you associate with being creative? What things were you doing when you felt most creative in the past? How can you incorporate those into your work routine to signal your brain that it is time to be creative?

## Ha-Ha Aha

People prepare for physical activity by warming up with stretching exercises that increase their flexibility. Have you thought of preparing for mental activity by stretching your brain increasing its flexibility?

Humor can serve as a metal warm up because it forces you to be mentally flexible. For example, Can you tell me how long cows should be milked? . . . The same as short ones.

In order to find that joke funny, you have to switch from one meaning of a word to another meaning of the same word. In the cow joke, your definition of long has to switch from duration of time to the animal's size. Your thoughts have to change direction.

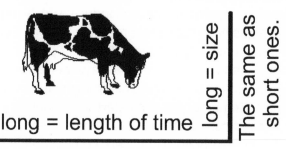

long = length of time     long = size     The same as short ones.

## Can you tell me how long cows should be milked?

Humor forces you to make new connections between words and concepts. It forces you to change the image you have. That same type of flexibility is just what is required for generating new ideas.

"In fact, humor and creativity are almost synonymous," said Randy Munson. "A dictionary definition of humor is 'the mental faculty of discovering, expressing, or appreciating ludicrous or absurdly incongruous elements in ideas, situations, happenings, or acts.' If you were to take the words 'ludicrous or absurdly' out of the definition of humor, you would have a definition of creativity. One way to be creative is to associate elements not normally combined."

Dr. Joel Goodman, director of the Humor Project, refers to this as the Ha-Ha Aha connection.

This has been verified by research. Experiments have been done where students were divided into three groups. One group listened to classical music. The second group listened to a tape of a motivational speaker. The third group listened to a tape of a stand up comedian. Afterwards all three groups were given standard creativity tests. The group that had listened to comedy scored highest on the test.

The research by Dr. William Fry is another indication of the link between humor and creativity. According to Dr. Fry, preschool children laugh or smile an average of four hundred times a day, but adults only laugh or smile an average of fifteen times a day. Not only do people use less humor as they age, but they also become less creative. It is estimated that 90 percent of preschoolers are highly creative, but only 2 percent of people over the age of eight are classified as highly creative. A correlation does not prove a cause and effect, but the two declines seem to be linked.

According to Jordon Ayan, "The sound of laughter shocks people out of automatic pilot so that they can become fully aware. Humor is often the starting gun that tells people it is OK to imagine fun, or weird, thoughts—exactly what you need to trigger an association or idea that breaks down a creative block. In fact, some of the most interesting ideas come from making connections between blips of thought and associations after hearing a joke, story, pun, or odd twist on a situation or event."

Humor forces you to look at something from a new perspective. You see it a little differently. It jolts your thinking off its normal track into new directions. It can create new metaphors. For example, on the April 25, 1939, broadcast of the *Fibber McGee and Molly* radio program, Fibber got a pair of glasses. The Old Timer, played by Bill Thompson, asked him, "When did you start wearing skepticals?" That is a funny line, but it also works as a metaphor. Spectacles help you see things clearer and inspect them more closely, which is exactly what a skeptic wants to do. That joke inspired a bit I sometimes use. When a skeptic asks to inspect one of my magic props, I take off my glasses and hand my spectacles to them so they can see the prop better.

I use humor as a mental warm up by reading the comic strips in the morning newspaper before I start any writing project. I can tell that it has made a big difference in my creativity. Another thing I do is listen to audio tapes of classic radio comedy programs while driving to a performance. I've noticed that I have consistently better ad-libs and audience interactions following those humor sessions.

Besides increasing your mental flexibility, humor aids creativity in another way. Physical or emotional stress inhibits creativity by either blocking access to your unconscious mind or making your brain work so rapidly in a "fight or fright" response that ideas don't have a chance to incubate. The research into the link between humor and health has proven that humor effectively counters stress. By using humor to reduce stress during the day, you free your mind to be more effective in generating ideas.

American businesses have discovered that humor is efficient and effective. They are consciously introducing humor to increase creativity and productivity. These efforts range from humorous signs posted throughout the work place to humor bulletin boards to joke-telling sessions beginning staff meetings to rooms set aside for collections of humorous materials. For example, Kodak, in Rochester, New York, has a humor room.

Combining humor and creativity is not new. Leonardo da Vinci was known as a humorist and he recorded some of his jokes in his notebooks along with his scientific observations and philosophical musings.

Thomas Edison would add jokes to the journals being kept by his research assistants to provide them with humor.

Here are some suggestions for starting your own humor collection. Become a "cut up" by clipping cartoons out of the newspaper. Watch for bloopers, humorous headlines and photo captions, and funny advertisements. Buy comic strip compilations or joke and cartoon calendars. Regularly check the humor sections of book and video stores for items that appeal to you. Collect old time radio programs. Subscribe to an on-line joke service.

What type of humor do you most enjoy? How can you collect it? How can you use humor to give you a mental warm up before working on new ideas?

# Play

According to Kurt Hanks and Jay Parry, "A person might be able to be play without being creative, but sure can't be creative without playing."

This was confirmed in the 1970s in research done at Berkeley by MacKinnon. Tests showed that highly creative people were no more intelligent than less creative ones. However, highly creative people took longer to study problems and played with them more. MacKinnon described the creative mood as being "more childlike."

According to Jordon Ayan, "Play eases you into a state of mind that contains many of the elements you need to be creative—curiosity, imagination, experimentation, fantasy, speculation or what if, role playing, and wonder."

Play also removes pressure. What you are doing is not IMPORTANT. It doesn't matter what the results are. If the results are something you can use, that is great. But if they are not successful, that is okay, it is just play. When you are playing, you are having fun. That is its purpose. Since the results aren't going to be judged, you stop being self-conscious. Failure doesn't have any consequence so you can risk doing anything. Like humor, play counters the stress that so often blocks creativity.

Let me give you a word of caution about playing with magic props. When you first receive a magic trick, you have to start in the explorer role to gather vital information. I purchased a gimmick for producing silks through mail order. As I unpacked it, I discovered there was a piece of tissue paper under a lever. I removed the tissue, and played around with the gimmick a little before I looked at the directions. The first line of the directions was, "Before you do anything, carefully study how the tissue paper is positioned under the lever. This is how the silk must be loaded in order to pop into view properly." I hadn't paid attention to the tissue paper, and never was able to get the gimmick to work to my satisfaction. I've purchased other tricks where a delicate thread connected parts of an apparatus. Handling it in the wrong manner would have broken the thread and prevented it from working. (This is one reason you should never touch another entertainer's props without their permission. There may be a delicate set up that you aren't aware of.)

However, once you know how a prop works and how to avoid damaging it, don't be too concerned about how it should be used. Switch to your artist role. Play around with the prop. Find out what else it can be used for.

When I was growing up, I didn't have a lot of money to spend on props for my magic hobby. That turned out to be an advantage. I would play around with the props that I did have, inventing new uses for them. I didn't perform most of my new routines for an audience other than my family. I used the props as toys that I played with for my own enjoyment.

My first magic set had a Ball and Vase with a blue ball. A Ball and Vase is shaped like an eggcup with a lid. There is a hollow half ball gimmick. If you leave the gimmick setting on the base when you lift the lid, it looks like the vase contains a ball. If you lift the gimmick when you raise the lid, the vase is empty creating the illusion the ball has vanished. The trick came with a complete ball you could put someplace else to reproduce.

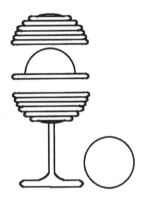

Ball And Vase

The magic set also had a Multiplying Ball effect with red balls. A standard Multiplying Ball effect has three solid balls and a hollow half ball shell that fits over the other balls.

The Ball and Vase is created to perform a vanish, but I used it for a transformation. I discovered that one of the red balls would fit under the blue half ball in the vase. I showed the blue ball in the vase. I covered it. When I uncovered it, the ball had turned red. Sometimes I used the vase transformation as an opening to my Multiplying Balls routine.

I also discovered that the solid blue ball would fit into the red shell from my Multiplying Balls set. That meant I could show the ball with the shell towards the audience making it appear red. I covered the ball with my hand, secretly removed the shell, and moved my hand to show the ball had turned blue. I combined the two color changing tricks to make it appear that the balls had traded places.

At Easter, our baskets included little chenille baby chicks. I discovered that one of those chicks would fit under the gimmick in my vase. So, I referred to the ball as an egg, covered it while it incubated, and then uncovered it revealing the egg had hatched into a chick. Other times I would call the ball a seed, and transform it into a small flower.

Such playfulness is natural for children, but adults seem to loose that ability. I try to revive that when I am working on a new routine.

One of the things I do is fidget with props, getting the feel for them, and turning them in different directions. Dena Pariano asked me to help her create a routine for her Pom Pom Stick. A Pom Pom Stick is a commercial effect that looks like a stick with strings running through either end. One string is short, and the other is longer. Each string has pom poms attached to the ends. If you pull on the short string, it grows longer, while the other string becomes shorter. You keep pulling on the strings, changing their sizes, and then prove that there isn't any connection between the two. A Pom Pom Stick is normally held horizontally.

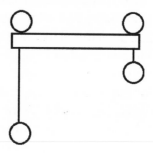

While I was talking to Dena, I turned the stick so it was vertical. The strings reminded me of arms and legs. That inspired a routine that worked well for Dena. She turned her Pom Pom Stick into a clown doll. She purchased a vinyl clown doll head, vinyl hands, and vinyl shoes from a craft store. The diameter of her stick was just right for the doll head to slip onto. She replaced the pom poms with hands and feet. Then she wrote a storyline about the anklebone being connected to the shinbone, and the shinbone being connected to . . . In performance, as she gave an anatomy lecture, she kept changing the lengths of the clown's arms and legs as her character became more and more confused about connections.

The first time I saw a magic effect called D'Lite was at the first *Angel Ocasio's Northwest Comedifest.* D'Lite is a translucent plastic thimble shaped like your thumb with a battery and a red light inside. When you press on the tip, the end glows. I bought one, and I think I drove the other festival participants crazy by playing incessantly with it. I saw somebody make a ladybug out of a 260 balloon. I picked it up, and discovered if that I pushed the thumb tip against the back of the balloon it looked like the bug's tail was glowing. I announced it was a lightning bug. I created my own version of Paul Jerome's blinking neon heart by inflating a heart balloon and pushing on the back with the tip to make it blink. The tables in the hotel restaurant had votive candles in red holders. When the waitress came, I told her the dim lights made it hard to read the menu. Using my thumb and forefinger, I plucked a little light from the candleholder and held it above the menu while I read my selection for dinner. Angel Ocasio and Albert Alter were emceeing the Open Mike as their characters Bud and Bud. I plucked some light from Albert's shoulder, and announced it was a Bud light. As people were leaving at night, I plucked some light from one taillight and carried it over to another car to turn on their taillight. I just had fun with my new toy. I wasn't concerned with whether the things I did would work in performance. I was enjoying seeing how many ways I could use it. At the end of the day, I had a list of thirty possible uses for the D'Lite. I've never used most of them since then, but I still perform the blinking heart in my act. I've heard that some people are using other ideas they saw me play with that day.

Even if I had never used any of those ideas, the day would still have been useful. Your physical muscles are strengthened by exercise, and your mental abilities are strengthened by exercise. Using the D'Lite to inspire the creation of new ideas improved my ability to generate ideas.

The playful approach works with other types of props. When I got cigar boxes, Randy Pryor encouraged me to play with them first. One of the things I did was throw and catch them in a regular cascade pattern. That led to some interesting discoveries that aren't currently part of my act, but that I might add in the future. When I first mastered plate spinning, I learned how to transfer a plate to other objects. I began playing around to see how many different things I could transfer it to. I discovered that a conical birthday party hat will support a spinning plate. So, sometimes during birthday party shows, I will transfer a plate to the tip of the guest of honor's hat. That is a great photo opportunity for the parents.

When I created the golf routine that I performed in circuses, I took a golf club and a rubber ball to a park. I just had fun experimenting with all the different ways I could hit it. For example, missing the ball on the swing, but hitting it when I brought the club back, sending the ball off behind me. I got down aiming my putt by sighting along the golf club, which reminded me of the position a pool player assumes. I used the golf club as a cue stick and sank the ball that way. Only a few of the moves that I experimented with are part of the finished routine, but the club cue is how I conclude the routine.

We are loosing the ability to play in our culture. People fill every moment with work. A movement called Take Back Your Time has begun in Seattle and is spreading through the United States. The emphasis is on finding ways to spend less time working and more time on those things that make life enjoyable. Technology was supposed to make our life easier giving us more leisure time to enjoy. Instead, laptops and cell phones have made it possible for people to take their work with them everywhere they go. We had a friend who complained about the stress from his work. We invited him to go with us to the beach for a day on one of his days off. Instead of relaxing and forgetting about work, he spent most of his time on his cell phone talking to people at work.

How can you take time off from things that you have to do? What activities do you enjoy? How can you find time to play?

# Delay Judgement

John Kao said, "Allow ideas to develop by keeping possibilities open. It may be the second, third, or even fiftieth idea that clicks; Keeping the process open and avoiding premature closure are crucially important. Because creative work is exploratory, it deserves suspension of disbelief in the early stages. Bottom line: Reserve skepticism and doubt until assessment time."

"Suspending your disbelief" is a theatrical term that many business leaders have applied to creativity. In the theater, that means as an audience member you know what is happening on stage isn't real, but you voluntarily suspend that knowledge and pretend that it is real. For example, when watching a production of *Miss Saigon*, you know that the actress playing Kim does not actually shoot herself, but you willingly forget that and are affected emotionally as if she really has committed suicide so her child will be taken to the United States. In business, that means you know an idea might not be useable, but you voluntarily suspend that knowledge and pretend that it will work. In both cases, you know it is only a temporary condition. In *Miss Saigon*, you aren't shocked when the actress comes back to life in order to take her curtain bow. In creativity, you know you will eventually evaluate your ideas and implement the ones you think are most appropriate.

If you are working on a magic routine, don't worry about how you are going to perform it yet. In the artist role, figure out what the ideal routine would look like. Later, you will create a method of accomplishing that.

According to magician George Sands, "A scientist or an inventor has an idea of what he'd like to solve. He has a goal. You have an impossible dream. You outline the target. You work at it. There are failures, but there are accomplishments. As a child, I would see a magician do something. I didn't know how he did it. I wanted to know. So, I made up a method. Some of my methods were inferior, some were as good, some were identical, and some were superior. In later years, I realized the magician gave me an idea—a goal. Because I had seen it done, I knew it was possible. At this stage, I projected a further thought. What is it the audience would like to see that would prove you are a real magician? So I sat down and wrote out a routine, that I had no idea how to do. In some instances, I solved it immediately. In some instances, it took years. And in some instances, I never solved it."

Your artist is the role that gives you the goal. I created a routine I call the Hobo's Dream that is a version of a classic magic act called the Miser's Dream. I will describe it more fully later. To start I decided what the plot would be. I didn't consider how it would be accomplished. I just wrote the story that would be told. Then I switched back to the Explorer role to research possible magic methods.

Do whatever it takes to silence your Judge until after your Artist has had a chance to finish its work. When I first started writing magazine articles, I wrote the original version out by hand. The ideas just flowed. Then I would edit it later, type a revision, edit it a second time, and retype it. When I began working on a computer, I found that I would edit as I worked. Because I could see the words I had just written, and editing it was easy, I would do it then. I knew that wasn't the most creative way to write, but I didn't seem to be able to break the habit. When I started using a program with grammar check, the problem increased because my computer prompted me to stop and change what I had written. The flow of ideas slowed to a trickle.

Then I read a suggestion by Tom Wujec. He said, "If you write at a word processor, turn off the computer monitor and just type ideas in as fast as you can. Don't look back. Don't stop to check for spelling. Just let your words come freely."

Wujec's method proved to be very freeing. I discovered that I could work a lot faster by getting the ideas down, and then coming back to edit it later. If I thought of an alternate way to word something while doing my first draft, I kept going and simply wrote the second version right then. It was easy to come back later, select the version I preferred and delete the other. I was amazed by how few mistakes I made when I couldn't see what I had typed, and how quickly my spell checker helped me find and correct them.

For some parts of this book, I went back to my original method of working. I took notes and did my rough draft writing by hand using a pen. I discovered that even using a pencil made it too easy to make changes, tempting me to slip into the Judge mode of thinking.

When Norman Lear wants to take notes of ideas he dictates them into a tape recorder. He said, "It will get me into a fair start, without pages that call my attention to them, and without sentences that are there for me to rewrite."

What can you do to silence your Judge so that your Artist has a chance to continue working? How can you preserve ideas without editing them at the time? What techniques will work for you?

## Embrace Wild Ideas

Delaying judging your ideas keeps the flow of new ones coming. Also, an idea you can't use may contain the seed for another useable idea. Being open to any idea, no matter how wild, allows those seeds to grow. Shallcross said, "The far out idea can be tempered later or refined into possibly becoming the answer being sought. They offer the new twist, the freshness of approach, the novelty of another way."

Dr. Joel Goodman advises, "Give yourself permission to engage in nonsense trusting that sense will not be far behind."

When I was working at Raging Waters, I went to a Chinese art exhibition at the Los Angeles Art Museum. That inspired an idea for an elaborate large-scale Oriental style illusion show with a cast of twelve performers. I drew a sketch of a permanent stage with a waterfall curtain. I knew the idea was crazy. The cost of building the stage was more then the park would invest. I did not have the time or money to build the illusions. I did not have the experience to direct such an elaborate show. I scaled down the idea and eliminated the Oriental style. I submitted a proposal and a design for a stage. The park built a small stage that was a simplified version of my design, approved hiring one assistant, and purchased two small stage illusions for my use. The assistant did not last long, but the show was enough of a success that a year later they built me a larger permanent stage and provided backstage storage for my props. That was unusual because storage space for any department at the park was rare. I appeared on that stage for several years. That dream of a large illusion show started the chain of events that resulted in a show that I was proud of and that was very popular with the regular guests.

## The Audience As Artist

Entertainers have an ally in generating ideas. According to comedian Joe E. Brown, "The best comedy is that which the audience itself helps to build. The experienced comedian is always on the lookout for the hints and suggestions that come to him through audience reaction."

Audience comments and challenges can inspire new ideas. I was handing out coloring pages with my picture on them at a birthday party. A little girl said, "If you could color one of those in by magic that would really be something." I couldn't do it as an impromptu routine. However, I thought that was a good idea. I know many possible methods of doing that. I finally decided upon using a method known as a Visual Painting. I constructed one that corresponded to my coloring page. For years, that was a highlight of my act. (I have since converted my visual painting over to another routine.)

At another party, there were eight girls and three boys. I decided to make napkin roses for each of the girls. Sometimes boys ask for roses when they see them. The roses are fascinating, and some boys want to keep them. Other boys give them to their mothers. After all the girls had their roses, the first boy said, "I want a rocket ship." I guessed that a bud and stem without a leaf might look like a rocket. I made that and he was content with it. The next boy wanted a racecar. I twisted several roses together into something that might possibly be a cockpit with four wheels. The boy was content with that although I didn't think it was too successful. The third boy wanted a turtle. I succeeded in making a turtle that looked good. So that I wouldn't forget, I practiced making turtles when I arrived home. I've never made another rocket or racecar, but turtle has now become a permanent part of my repertoire. I don't make many turtles, but they have been a great success in the right situations. (See Creativity for Entertainers volume 3 for directions on how to make a napkin rose and a napkin turtle.)

My friend Rick De Lung plays Stump, the Clown when he does balloon sculptures at birthday parties and company picnics. He challenges the kids to request a sculpture he can't make. Each child must ask for something different. No duplicates are allowed. At one picnic, a woman who had moved to Southern California from the state of Maine asked for a lobster. Rick managed to make one that satisfied the lady. The idea intrigued him. After he got home, Rick began working on perfecting a balloon lobster. He entered his lobster in the "multiple balloon sculpture competition" at the 1991 Western Region Clown Association Convention, and won Second Place. He repeated the effort in the 1992 World Clown Association Convention in Las Vegas and won the Gold Medal.

I incorporate chalk talks into my performances. It is a type of act that was very popular in vaudeville. A chalk talk is a cartoon that transforms in some way. For example, you print the word cat and then add some lines to turn it into a picture of a cat. I have several that I have practiced and use repeatedly. Sometimes, a child will request something different. A girl asked me for a picture of a horse. I had never done that before. I came up with something that looked good. I went home and refined the design. It is now one of my most popular drawings.

Begin by printing the word "HORSE" like this

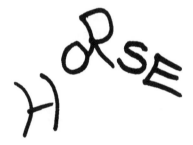

Then finish drawing the head of the horse.

Besides presenting challenges, audience members sometimes like to predict what will happen. In one routine, I take a handkerchief covered with stains, spray it with a bottle labeled "Spot Remover," and place it in a drawstring laundry change bag. One day a boy predicted, "The spots will come off on the inside of the bag!" That struck me as a possible addition to what I do which is remove the handkerchief to reveal that the stains are gone and in their place are holes their shape. If what the audience predicts is better than what you do, use their idea in future shows.

Questions asked by audience members can also spark ideas. At Raging Waters, I was doing a walk-a-round with a hot dog in a bun placed into an invisible dog harness. Kids started asking his name. Since I hadn't named him, they suggested some. I decided on "Frank" and had a dog tag made which says, "Frank The Hot Dog".

Another walk-a-round I used at Raging Waters was a cage with some type of bird visual pun in it. One week I had a letter "J" painted sky blue. That was my blue jay.

Blue Jay

A man stopped me, and said, "Charlie, your blue jay looks a little pale. What is wrong with him?" Since I performed silently, I wrote him a note asking him what he thought might be wrong. Suddenly I was surrounded by people discussing why my bird was so pale. They decided that he must be love sick, and needed a girlfriend. One lady suggested an "O-riole." I liked that idea. I could have made a big letter "O" for the perch, which I think she was visualizing. Instead, the next week, I had a package of Oreo cookies sitting on the perch of my cage.

I liked the concept of asking questions to draw out the creativity of my audience. Questions draw them in and let them become involved. At Raging Waters, I attached an oversized badminton shuttlecock to the perch. I prepared a note that said, "This is my birdie. What should I name him? Or is he a she?" I got some great responses to that. One lady said, "It's a he, because if it was a she it would be a shuttlehen." A little girl suggested, "His name should be Rudolph because he has a red nose."

Birdie

Sometimes when I am performing, an audience member will make a humorous comment. Often, they are just showing off for their friends. Other times they are playing along with me. If their comment gets a good laugh, I lead the audience in applauding them, and then I pause to write it down. That flatters them, and it draws a second laugh. It also prevents me from forgetting what they said. I let them get the attention at that performance, and then I add the line to my repertoire and use it at my other performances.

Each of my shows is a little bit different because the audience is different. Fanny Brice said, "Your audience gives you everything you need. There is no director who can direct you like an audience."

In my **Tramp Tradition Show** I recreate the types of routines that would have been used by famous or significant tramp clowns from the past 125 years. A pen and ink illustration of each clown is displayed using an overhead projector. When I get to Emmett Kelly, who performed a chalk talk act, I demonstrate some trick cartoons. I have prepared transparencies for each cartoon I will perform. As I draw the cartoons on a newsprint pad, the prepared cartoons are projected so everybody in the audience can see them. The person running the projector switches when what I have drawn matches the next transparency. Normally, the person doing this is seated in front of the stage where they can easily see what I am doing. At the 2003 Glorybound Clowns' **Wild Winter Workshop**, that person was seated on the stage where they could not see my drawing pad. I tried to turn when it was time to switch the transparencies so she could see what I had drawn. At one point, I could tell from the audience reaction that she was having difficulty. When I glanced at her, I saw a momentary expression of frustration. She switched to a deadpan as soon as she realized I was looking at her. I had not been aware of how difficult it had been for her, but the audience response had directed my attention to her. I had to respond to their concern. I put down the pad, went over, and massaged her shoulders a moment like a trainer working on a boxer between rounds. It was my way of letting her know she was doing okay and giving her a moment to recover from her frustration. It also got a nice laugh from the audience.

Emmett Kelly

In the same performance, I did another Emmett Kelly bit. I wandered through the audience nibbling on a head of cabbage. Then I would see a beautiful lady, and stare at her longingly as I continued eating cabbage. Finally, I would offer her some. I had done that with two different women. When I offered some cabbage to a third woman, she grabbed the entire head of cabbage. I had never had anybody do that before. I sighed, and let her keep it. As I moved away from her, I felt the audience sigh. I realized that was the natural ending for that particular performance. It was emotionally right for that audience. It didn't get a laugh, but it touched their heart because it made me sympathetic.

A few years ago, I was putting some scarves into a bag that I was going to transform into a banner. A little girl came up and gave me a doll she had been holding. I put the doll in the bag with the scarves. When her doll vanished, she looked concerned, and I heard a murmur in the audience. I knew right away that I had made a mistake. As quickly as possible, I reproduced the doll and returned it to her.

Every performance that I do is different from any other. That is because each one has a new director. I listen to the audience, watch their expressions, and follow their direction for what is right in that particular circumstance.

How can you allow the audience to become involved in your performances? How can you turn their suggestions into material for use in future performances? How can you use the audience as your director? How can you respond to them? How can they give you ideas for improvised moments in your show?

> *"The best way to get a good idea is to get a lot of ideas."—Linus Pauling, Nobel chemist.*

# What Is It?

## Exercises

1. Choose a common object. Now make a list of fifty unusual uses for that object. For example, if your object is a drinking glass, you might write "broken sofa leg replacement" or "pattern for drawing circles" or "emergency stethoscope." Don't worry about how practical or realistic the use is. Just imagine fifty ways.

   This is a standard creativity exercise. I was assigned it often in school. I did it in art classes, theater design classes, and writing classes.

   When I did this exercise for the first time, it took me several days to complete a list of fifty potential uses. After I graduated from college, I would do this exercise on my own sometimes just to exercise my mind. I got to the point where I could do it in about twenty minutes. Take the length of time that you need to complete it. You will experience what kind of creative process you currently use.

   After you have completed your list, take a few minutes to write down your experiences and reactions while doing the exercise. This will help you discover concepts that you can use in other projects.

2. Make a list of fifty objects that are similar to a dowel rod.

3. A related group exercise is to form a circle of from five to twelve people. Take a common object, for example a balloon, and pass it around the circle. When it comes to each person, they have to use it briefly as if it is something else. One person might use it as a crystal ball to tell a

fortune. The next person might put it on their shoulder and announce, "Two heads are better than one."

Don't go in order around the circle. If you do that, the people on the opposite side of the circle relax because they know they don't have to think yet. By going in a random order, everyone has to be thinking all the time. If the object comes to you more than once, you get a second opportunity to use it as another object.

During a class, I like to have my students do this exercise with two or three different objects.

At the beginning of a class in creativity, I ask how many people think they are creative. Usually, only a few people raise their hand. After doing this exercise, I ask again, and everyone raises their hand because they experienced their creativity during this exercise.

## Applications

## Creating New Material

At the 1987 *Laugh-Makers Conference*, Cathy Gibbons and I produced five different variety shows in five days. The shows were all open to the public. The cast of each show was a mixture of conference staff and participants. It seemed like every clown and magician, who performed that week, handed a magic wand to a child, and the wand broke. Some of the performers accused the children of breaking their wand. They tried to make light of it, but some of the children took it seriously. Parents complained that they were tired of that practical joke being played repeatedly on children. The biggest laugh of the series of shows came when a child, who had seen several of the shows, restored the wand and handed it back to the magician. Of course, it fell apart when the child let go so the magician was caught in his own trick.

The basic idea of the breakaway wand is a good one. A breakaway wand is made from plastic segments. The segments have a hole running through the center. The segments are threaded onto a cord. One end of each segment has a round bump. The other end has a round depression. The bumps fit into the depressions when the segments are end to end. This prevents them from sliding sideways. The end pieces have caps that screw on. The caps cover the ends of the cord, which are knotted. By moving the knots, you can adjust the tension on the cord. One segment of the wand is slotted. When it is slipped onto the cord, it takes up the slack in the cord pulling the segments close together so the wand appears rigid. When the slotted piece is removed, there is enough slack for the segments to move away from each other and the wand appear limp. Breakaway wands are sold in magic and novelty stores.

Breakaway Wand Cross Section

Breakaway Wand with Slotted Piece Maintaining Tension

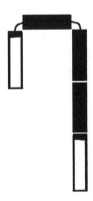

Breakaway Wand Without Slotted Piece

You don't have to use it the same way as everyone else. First, you can transform it into other objects. Second, you can cause it to break when you are handling it. That makes you the object of the humor, not a volunteer from the audience.

Look at the list you made of things that are similar to a dowel rod. Each of those items could be a potential breakaway prop.

You may be able to turn a standard breakaway wand into a different object. For example, for an artist routine I made a pencil out of a breakaway wand. I attached a section of dowel rod to one end of the wand. I carved the dowel rod into a point and used a pencil to draw the lead onto the dowel. I glued a piece of pink eraser to the other end of the wand. I purchased enamel paint from a model shop and painted the wand yellow. Finally, I wrapped some duct tape around the joint between the wand and the eraser to simulate the metal sleeve holding the eraser. Most performers discard the slotted gimmick that comes with the wand and use their fingers to control the tension. I use the slotted piece with the pencil to maintain the tension and keep the pencil rigid until I am ready for the pencil to break. That allows me to hold the pencil naturally. During the performance, I act like I am starting to draw with the pencil, and then it breaks because I pressed down too hard.

Breakaway Pencil

I have also made a breakaway spoon and a breakaway paintbrush by altering breakaway magic wands. What items on your list could be made from a breakaway wand?

Long hollow objects can be gimmicked like a wand. I use a breakaway club in my juggling act.

Charlie With Breakaway Club

I cut a one-piece juggling club into segments, and made wood plugs similar to the ends of the breakaway wand. I made a slotted gimmick out of a piece of dowel rod. It is anchored to the end of the club with a piece of fishing line. The gimmick allows me to start juggling with the club. When I knock the gimmick loose, the club seems to fall apart in mid-air. (The anchor line keeps the gimmick from flying away and hitting somebody.) Since I start using the club, it is more surprising when it comes apart. Below is a diagram showing the construction of the club. What items on your list can be gimmicked similar to a wand?

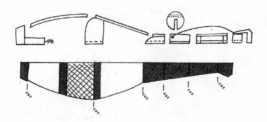

A solid object can be turned into a breakaway prop by cutting it and putting a hinge on one side. If you hold the item with the hinge on top, it will remain rigid. If you turn it so the hinge is on the bottom, it will bend right there. In my juggling act, I use a tennis racket gimmicked in this manner. It is based on an idea by Joe March in the February 1947 issue of **Juggler's Bulletin**.

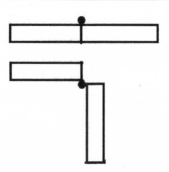

You can cut the object into as many pieces as you want just as long as all the hinges are on the same side. The more cuts that you use the more the prop will flop around when it is turned over. I have used this method to create a breakaway juggling ring.

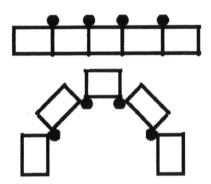

What objects from your list could be gimmicked in this manner?

We usually don't think of a piece of rope as a potential breakaway prop. However, there is a commercially marketed magic prop called a Stiff Rope. It is essentially a breakaway dowel rod inside a rope sleeve. It is just used in reverse. Instead of starting rigid and becoming limp, it starts flexible and becomes rigid.

Jim Kleefeld did this exercise in a class that I taught at one of the *Laugh-Makers Conference*. The next year he did a hilarious act at the conference where almost every object that he picked up was a breakaway prop.

## Use in Performance

While this exercise teaches you a lot about creativity in general, it has a direct application to being a variety artist. By transforming your props and using them as different objects, you create a playful atmosphere. It is common for a juggler to use a juggling club as a telescope when looking for a volunteer and then use it as a hand held microphone while interviewing their new assistant. Other jugglers have used a juggling club as if it was a liquor bottle, a telephone, and a pirate's peg leg.

Here is another example of this type of performance. In the *Vakerie* edition of Cirque du Soleil, one of the comedy characters, takes two light bulbs and uses them as maracas, popped eyes, and teardrops running down his face.

Balloon artists often use this technique. For example, making a figure eight out of a balloon is a step used in many sculptures. The entertainer than takes this shape and uses it as if it is a duck's bill, pair of glasses, and other objects before they go on to the next step of the sculpture.

It is possible to turn this into a little play by using the balloon to quickly turn from one character to another. The entertainer could play all the parts in a melodrama by holding the balloon under their nose and pushing down on the lobes to make the villain's mustache, putting the balloon above their head for the heroine's hair bow, and holding it in front of their collar for the hero's bow tie.

The Open Sesame clown troupe sometimes makes the exercise a part of their shows. They take an object and begin using it as if it is something else. Then they bring up an audience volunteer, give them the object, and wait to see what the volunteer does with it. No matter what the volunteer does, the clowns lead the audience in applauding them.

## Comic Inventiveness and Mistaken Identity

These exercises are related to two different comedy techniques, Comic Inventiveness and Mistaken Identity.

In Comic Inventiveness, the character has a problem and finds an unusual solution. A clown may break the leg off a chair, and use a drinking glass to replace it. In a cartoon by Bernhardt, a couple finds a clever way to screw in a light bulb. The man stands on a piano stool holding a light bulb over his head while his wife spins the seat.

In Mistaken Identity, the character uses an object in an unusual way because he does not realize the object's true identity. For example, in the "Adam" comic strip by Brian Basset, Adam can't figure out why he can't get the bathtub clean. In the final frame, he discovers that the container of cleanser that he has been using is really Parmesan Cheese. Mistaken Identity can establish a character as either being slow witted or simply being nearsighted like Mr. Magoo.

# Incubation

Another creativity paradox is that it requires work and discipline, but it also requires not doing anything and freedom.

Randy Munson said, "I have asked tens of thousands of people in audiences around the world, 'what were you doing at the time you got your last really creative idea?' The backgrounds, experiences, and creative ideas of these people were extremely diverse, and the activities these people were engaged in when they got their ideas were varied. However, there is one amazing consistency. I have never had anyone tell me they get their great creative ideas when they sit at their desk and work really hard."

Why do those ideas come when you aren't working? While you are working on an idea, your conscious mind is in control. When you do something else to keep your conscious mind occupied, it relaxes and your subconscious has a chance to work. It is more effective at generating ideas because it is uncritical and combines elements at random without considering their practicality.

Also, most of your memory is stored in your subconscious. Cognitive scientists say only about 1 percent of your memory is accessible to your rational conscious mind. That is why you can suddenly remember something you haven't thought about in years. Although it wasn't part of your conscious memory, it was still stored in your subconscious until something happened to make it accessible. When you let your subconscious work on ideas it has access to all the memories and knowledge stored there.

For one of the chapters of this book I wanted to use some examples of how I have put things to other use. I knew that I had used that creativity technique many times. However, when I was writing that chapter, I couldn't think of any examples. For two weeks, I looked at my notes for that chapter every day and tried to write something, but didn't have any ideas. Then I set that chapter aside, and purposely did not work on this book for three days. Suddenly the ideas began flowing, and I had many more examples than I could use.

## Patience

Arnold Glasgow said, "You get the chicken by hatching the egg, not by smashing it."

To come up with the best ideas, you need to let the project incubate and see what will hatch. You have to be patient with yourself and the creative process. This is another place where your opinion of your creativity plays a role. People who think they are not creative are impatient. If they can't come up with an idea right away, they think that is just confirmation that they can't create anything. So, they give up. People who think they are creative are patient. They think that if they work long enough they will be able to come up with a good idea. So, they let the process continue and eventually they find a great idea.

Sometimes you have to let an idea incubate just because you aren't ready to use it yet. Creating a routine is like fitting together a jigsaw puzzle and you can't complete it without all the pieces. Sometimes a missing piece is an idea that makes everything come together, developing the necessary technical skill, learning a concept of showmanship, being inspired by a new experience, finding the right venue or opportunity, or changing your assumptions.

Since 1987, I had wanted to do a routine utilizing a spotlight and juggling balls that light up. I had seen some balls that contained a rechargeable battery, but didn't invest in them because they were expensive and I didn't have the opportunity to use them. At that time, most of my performances were on outdoor stages during the day. By the time I had a performance scheduled on an appropriate stage, the balls were no longer available. For many years I have performed "Staff On Stage" shows at Clown Camp®. Those shows were presented on a small stage without a spotlight. In 1999, the building the program normally used for shows was being remodeled, and the shows were moved to the University's large theater, which included a spotlight. That same year, I discovered a new type of lighted ball that was a great improvement over the earlier design. So, in 1999, the pieces came together and I debuted my spotlight routine. During the twelve years that the idea had been incubating it had evolved and grown. My skill as an entertainer had also improved. I had begun paying more attention to my use of music. The routine with the lighted balls was the first one I created with moves choreographed to a specific song. The routine I created and performed in 1999 was much better than what I could have done in 1987.

Sometimes you need time to assimilate what you have learned, either in terms of skills or concepts. I struggled with plate spinning off and on for several years. I would practice for months without making progress, get frustrated, and put the plate away. Then one day, I picked up the plate and spun it. Within an hour, I could start it spinning 80 percent of the time. Within a week, I had a short routine that I could add to my performances. What had happened? Since the last time I had practiced, my subconscious had made a vital connection that made learning to spin the plate possible. Now, when I work on a new routine, I maintain a daily practice schedule. After a month, or when I seem to have hit a plateau in progress, I'll set the routine aside and not work on it for a week or two. When I return to a regular schedule, I often experience a growth spurt because I've had time to assimilate what I had learned to date.

In 1977, I was touring as a clown with Circus Kirk. In keeping with the tramp clown stereotype, Charlie, my tramp character, was the victim in all the acts. One day, Doc Boas, the owner of the show, told me that the audience was tired of seeing Charlie loose all the time. I didn't understand what he meant. In 1980, I was touring with the Carson & Barnes Five-Ring Circus. All of my acts were done in a bumbling manner. I had written a bumbling juggling act, but hadn't developed the necessary skill to perform it. It takes more skill to do a good bumbling act than to do a serious juggling act. One of the juggling acts left the show near the end of the season. The managers knew I had been practicing juggling, so they asked me to substitute for the act. I performed it more as a straight act with some comedy bits. Two years later, I was touring with the intimate Funs-A-Poppin Circus. I did many acts where I got things wrong. My last act in the show was my juggling act. My parents attended a performance and overheard somebody in the audience exclaim, "Hurray! He can do something right." When I heard about that, the comment by Doc Boas suddenly made sense. People liked Charlie and wanted to see him succeed. They like to root for the underdog and see them win. I changed my concept of Charlie from a hopeless bungler to an idiot savant. He couldn't do much, but he could juggle because that was the one thing he had concentrated on learning. I discarded the assumptions I had been taught by others about the tramp characterization. It took me five years to understand what Doc meant, and to apply it to my performances.

## Multiple Projects

Have more than one project at a time. Then when you hit an obstacle, you can let it incubate by switching to another project. Thomas Edison performed some experiments with incandescent lights, but couldn't progress because an efficient enough vacuum pump had not been invented yet. So, he turned to working on improvements to the telegraph. While working on that, he discovered the principle that made the invention of the phonograph possible. By that time improvements in vacuum pumps made it possible for him to return to his work with the electric light. He set the phonograph aside while he spent ten years perfecting the incandescent light and inventing the electric distribution system that made it practical. Then he returned to perfecting the phonograph. According to Dean Keith Simonton, "most of history's great creators didn't just have their hands in one basket. They had lots of different things going on."

However, don't fill your life with projects that always keep you busy. It is important to rest your mind. When Edison moved to Florida he would sometimes go fishing without bait because he felt "sitting a spell" without doing anything was an important part of the creative process.

## Get Physical

Many people find that some type of physical activity helps the incubation process. It helps you shift from L-mode thinking to R-mode thinking. I'm working on this portion of the book in the spring. One of my spring chores is chipping branches that have fallen during the winter. I've gotten a lot of ideas for this book while running the chipper. It requires a little concentration, but doesn't demand my full attention. When I first started clowning, I was working as a janitor in a church. Some of my best ideas came while running the floor polisher.

When Mozart was struggling with a new composition, he would go for a walk. Sometimes he would walk several miles. Often during his walk he would visualize the entire composition. I follow his example and discover a lot of ideas while walking.

The physical activity keeps your rational mind just busy enough that it doesn't block your subconscious without being so busy thinking that you aren't receptive to ideas from your subconscious.

When you feel blocked in a creative project, instead of continuing to bang your head against the obstacle, take a break, do something physical, and let the block crumble itself. If you have just a brief time to let a project incubate, this is one of the best strategies.

What kind of physical activity do you enjoy? How can you incorporate that into your schedule when working on a project?

## Sleep On It

Going to sleep is another good way to incubate ideas. That is another time when your conscious mind relaxes allowing your subconscious free reign. Brain scans have shown that during the REM period of sleep, which is when you dream, there is no activity in the frontal area of the brain that is responsible for planning and reasoning. That means your mental control and inhibitions are blocked. While you are dreaming, uncensored and unmanaged images and ideas merge in unexpected ways. Dr. Pierce Howard suggests considering your dreams as a form of brainstorming. Some of my best ideas have been the result of dreams in the middle of the night.

Many people find that a siesta gives their creativity a great boost. This was one of Thomas Edison's favorite techniques. He would take frequent power naps. He would keep a pen and paper by his side so that he could write down ideas that occurred to him while he was going to sleep or waking up.

## Relaxation

Stress blocks creativity. Anything that counters stress will help boost creativity. Anything that helps you relax during your time of incubation will make you more creative. This may be different things for different people. I find sketching very relaxing, but I know other people find it very frustrating.

Repetitive actions tend to be relaxing. To me the rhythm of juggling is relaxing. Studies have shown that juggling can be a form of stress relief. Dr. Steve Allen Jr. teaches juggling to businessmen and health professionals. However, if you are struggling to learn to juggle it can be stressful. It becomes relaxing only after you have learned to do it and can fall into the proper rhythm without having to think about it.

Some people find other repetitive activities to be relaxing. For example, some people find that knitting relaxes them.

Something else that I find relaxing is to sit on the floor and play solitaire with a deck of cards. There is something about actually handling the cards that I find more relaxing than playing the game on a computer.

Music is something that can help people to relax. If you have time for only a brief break from a project, turning on some music can be very effective.

If a farmer keeps planting the same field constantly, the crop will eventually fail. The field's resources have been depleted. Refreshing a field by letting it lie fallow for a season is an important concept in agriculture. The same thing can happen mentally. If you are working on ideas all the time, you can deplete your resources. You need to refresh your mind by letting it lie fallow. By doing something relaxing and not work related you give your mind a chance to restore itself.

What is relaxing to you? How can you incorporate that into your work routine to allow your ideas to incubate and to counter the negative effects of stress?

## Proper Preparation

Edward Blakeslee said, "Your most brilliant ideas come in a flash, but the flash comes only after a lot of hard work. Nobody gets a big idea when he is not relaxed, and nobody gets a big idea when he is relaxed all the time."

Incubation seems to be most effective when you have completed the necessary research and have worked as hard as you can to find a solution without success. You have to lay an egg before there is anything in the incubator to hatch. You have to work to stock up the incubator.

To use a different analogy, when carbon is subjected to pressure over a long period, it turns into a diamond. You have to start with enough raw materials. Then there has to be the right amount of pressure applied over time. In creativity, in the Explorer role, you gather the raw material. During the Artist role, you put pressure on yourself to generate new ideas. During Incubation you allow time to turn your raw material into a diamond of an idea. You give your subconscious time to work on the problem. The more work you have done in preparation, the more material your subconscious has to work with.

Paul MacCready, inventor of the Gossamer Condor, said, "You have to get yourself immersed in the subject, and to a certain extent you need some good technical preparation in order to get started. Then, it if gets interesting to you, you start thinking about it at odd hours. Maybe you can't come up with a solution, and you forget about it for awhile, and suddenly while you are shaving you get a good idea."

## Utilize Deadlines

I've found that a realistic deadline helps me produce diamonds. It works in two ways. First, it reassures me that I have time to come up with ideas. I don't have to have one right now so there is time to let it incubate. However, it puts a little pressure on my subconscious. It keeps my subconscious engaged hunting for a solution instead of running off after some other scent. What has worked for me is to select a couple of significant performances each year. Then I pick something new I want to have ready to perform for each of those performances. Sometimes it is a routine that I have wanted to do for years, but just never committed myself to completing. For example, for twenty years I thought about creating a Miser's Dream routine where I would produce coins from the air. I was invited to perform my *Tramp Tradition Show* at the 2001 World Clown Association Convention. That show requires that I perform a magic routine that might have been performed by a tramp clown magician during the days of vaudeville. I had used other magic routines in previous performances of the show, but decided to use the Miser's Dream during that performance. I started working on the routine four months before the convention, and had it ready to present there right on schedule.

Often I find that my best ideas come just before the deadline. For a year, I was a Bible Study Fellowship children's leader. Each week I received a teaching outline and suggested activities. However, I was expected to find my own creative ways to present the lesson. Our class met on Monday nights. Although I worked all week on ideas, and presented some of them at a leader's meeting on Saturday morning, I would consistently discover my best ideas on Sunday evening and spend Monday making them a reality.

It is important that you use realistic deadlines. If you don't give yourself enough time, the pressure may interfere with your creativity. You will give up in frustration. However, if you set the deadline too far in the future you may loose interest and give up from boredom.

What kind of routine have you always wanted to do? Realistically, how long would it take to prepare it? What performances do you have scheduled? Select one of those performances, and use that as a deadline for having your routine ready.

## Visual Reminders

Another way to keep your subconscious working on the problem during the incubation period is with a visual reminder. Your subconscious uses images instead of words. Pictures and drawings are quickly perceived by the subconscious. Placing inspirational art where you will often see it reminds your subconscious of the task at hand.

A group of Disney Imagineers were assigned the task of designing a new water slide park for the Orlando Florida resort. There were some snow globes in the room where they were meeting for a brainstorm session. Eric Jacobson picked up a snow globe and commented that it was too bad they couldn't build a park inside one of them. Tim Kirk sketched a cartoon of an alligator skiing off a cliff. Jullie Svednsen did a drawing of a ski resort inside a snow dome. These two drawings were placed on a bulletin board where everybody could see them. They evolved into the idea for Blizzard Beach, a water slide park with a ski resort theme. The basic premise was that a snow resort had been built during a rare blizzard in Florida, but the return of normal warm weather melted the snow turning the ski runs into streams of water. The original drawings remained on the board to remind people of the concept. Gradually, other photographs, doodles, and inspirational drawings and paintings were added to the board. This allowed everyone involved to see everything at a glance which led to new associations and ideas. Then as progress was made on the project, the idea board became more organized. Eventually it became a storyboard looking like a page in a comic book with each panel taking you another step through the park and attractions.

When I was working on the design for my cowboy costume, I found a cartoon of Dennis the Menace in a cowboy outfit. I liked the emotion the drawing evoked, so I placed it on my bulletin board in my bedroom where I could see it every day.

Your inspirational art does not have to have a literal link to your project. It just has to remind you of the project and some quality you want to incorporate. In college, I worked on a production of Shakespeare's *The Tempest*. The costume designer posted a picture of a coral reef and a photo of a clamshell in the costume studio where everybody could see it. Many of the costume colors were chosen from the colors of the coral. The clamshell resulted in lots of pleats in the costumes. The scene designer for the same production used a painting of a storm at sea for his inspirational art. He felt the emotions of the painting were the same as those in the play. The set wasn't an identifiable wave, but many of the shapes echoed those in the painting.

If you are working on a project that has a theme or slogan, post that on a sign. If you are working on a gospel ministry program with a guiding verse, post that where you can see it. You don't have to actively work on ideas during the incubation process, but the reminder will keep your subconscious involved.

A good place to put your visual reminder is where you will see it just before going to sleep. I know several magicians that put a prop they want to find a use for on their night stand. This technique often results in insights during the night or in the morning.

What routines are you working on now? What visual images do you associate with it? What images evokes the emotions you want the routine to include? Where can you place that so that you see it frequently?

## Changing Perspective

Here is a picture of two trees.

Now, I've added a boat.

Now, I've added a bird.

Now, I've added a second bird.

Look at the picture again. Can you see the face of the Lady of the Lake?

As long as I directed your attention to the details that is what you saw. It wasn't until you changed your perspective and looked at the entire drawing that you saw the face.

When you begin working on a problem or a project, you focus on the details. When you take a break, and come back to it later, you have distanced yourself from those details. Often you can see more of the picture. You can see how the details relate to each other. Frequently, this new perspective allows you to see something entirely different from what you saw before.

After I write something, I carefully edit and proofread it. When I read it later, I am often surprised by the errors I find: typographical, structural, and in content. Why didn't I see them earlier? When I first finish the project, I assume that it says what I meant it to and I see what I expect to see. When I return to it later, I have forgotten what I thought was there and I am able to see what is actually there. Allowing a project to incubate during the planning stages allows you to forget or change your assumptions so you can take a fresh look at it again. As Steven Smith, a psychologist at Texas A&M University, said, "Fertile forgetting is a major factor in incubation."

According to Leonardo da Vinci, "It is also a very good plan every now and then to go away and have a little relaxation; for when you come back to the work your judgment will be surer, since to remain constantly at work will cause you to lose the power of judgment."

> *"The greatest geniuses sometimes accomplish more when they work less."—Leonardo da Vinci*

> *"Learn to pause . . . or nothing worthwhile will catch up to you."—Doug King*

# Illumination

## Eureka

Illumination is that "Eureka" moment when you are suddenly aware of a great idea. It may seem to come from nowhere, but it is actually the result of work your subconscious has been doing unseen. It wouldn't have occurred without the preparation you did providing your subconscious with something to work with.

Those moments come most often when your rational conscious mind is relaxed and receptive to listening to your subconscious. Some of my best ideas come to me during that period between sleep and complete wakefulness. My subconscious has worked on it during the night and while I am half-asleep the thoughts move from my subconscious to my conscious. I try to maintain that relaxed state as long as possible to let the idea fully blossom. Then I have to get up and write it down before I forget what it was.

Many people find that their moments of illumination come consistently during the same activity. I have read that many people experience it while taking a shower. For others, it is while driving a car. Dr. Seuss (Theodore Geisel) found that he would get many ideas while shaving. He kept an idea file that he referred to as the Shaving File.

The reason illumination happens consistently during certain activities is that it has become a self-fulfilling prophecy. A person associates that activity with moments of illumination, so they expect it to happen again. That puts them into the mental frame of mind that allows it to happen.

# Record Ideas

Leon McBryde says, "A short pencil is better than a long memory."

Leonardo da Vinci carried a notebook with him all the time to record ideas and observations as they occurred. Seven thousand pages of his notebooks still exist, and experts estimate that is about half of what he wrote during his lifetime.

Ideas can be fleeting. Nothing is as frustrating as knowing you have had a great idea, but not being able to remember what it was. I know that ideas can come anytime and anywhere, and if I don't write them down, they can quickly dissolve away. I keep small pads of paper everywhere: in my car, next to my bed, in the pocket of the coat I wear most often, near the phone, on my desk, and other places. I keep a few sheets of notebook paper tucked into my Bible.

If I wake up during the night with an idea, I find I can't go back to sleep until I've written it down. My conscious mind, trying to hold onto the idea, won't let me relax. Once it is in writing so I don't have to remember it, I can go back to sleep.

Just the act of writing something down helps lock it into your memory. Studies have shown that you forget what you hear within a few hours, you forget what you see within a few days, but you still remember what you write next week. In college, I took a class in effective ways to study and take tests. My instructor advocated taking notes as you read instead of using a highlighter because writing is such an effective memory aid. Printing your notes seems to work the best. Not only are they easier to read later, but they are also easier to remember.

If you know you tend to experience illumination in the same place, find a way to record those ideas.

Some people who get their ideas in the shower keep a grease pencil next to the shampoo. When an idea comes, they write it down on the tiles. After their shower, they transfer the idea to paper, and then they use a liquid cleaner to wipe off the wall.

People who tend to experience illumination in the car keep a small tape recorder handy so they can safely dictate their idea while driving.

If you are away from home when an idea comes, phone yourself and leave a message on your answering machine.

Carry 3x5 cards with you. They fit easily into a shirt pocket or a wallet.

Charlie "Chic" Thompson carries slips of paper the size of dollar bills in his wallet. This helps remind him that ideas are valuable and to enter them into his "idea bank."

Where does illumination tend to happen for you? How can you be prepared to record those ideas?

## Keep an Idea Bank

It doesn't do you any good to record ideas if you can never find them again. You need some way to store your ideas so that they are accessible.

Many entertainers utilize an idea journal to record their ideas. This can take a variety of forms. Some people like to use bound journals because it provides a sense of importance to the ideas. Some use a loose-leaf notebook. Some write on lined notebook paper, while others feel blank paper is more liberating. Other people use scrapbooks. This is for your use. Don't worry about rules or how it is going to look to others. Draw doodles of possible ideas, even when you aren't sure what the result will be. Cut out and paste in cartoons with possible skit ideas. Include your favorite jokes. Most often ideas are recorded in a journal in the order that you come up with them. There is no attempt at organization. There are disadvantages and advantages with this method. A disadvantage is that it can be difficult to find specific ideas when you need them. An advantage is that exploring the journal allows you to make connections between unrelated ideas that you wouldn't otherwise if the entries were segregated by topic. If you keep a journal, don't forget to review earlier entries frequently. Often a new idea combined with an old idea will generate a great idea.

Ideas can be stored in a computer and searched for by topic. I have found that this isn't always effective for me. Looking at ideas on a computer screen forces you to review them in order which shifts you into L-mode thinking. It also limits you to just what can be seen on the screen at any one time. Not only that, but since you get the results you ask for when you do a computer search you decrease the chance of serendipity revealing an unexpected idea. For this book, I wrote the rough draft, and put the pages in a notebook. Then as I did additional research, I entered the ideas into my computer and printed them out. I cut the ideas apart and paper clipped them to the appropriate page in the notebook. Then when I was ready for my next draft, I was able to spread the ideas out, see them all at once, decide how they related to each other, and move them around. Sometimes I shifted ideas to a completely different chapter.

Which method of storing ideas works best for you? How can you organize them so you can find them again? How can you review your ideas in a random order increasing the chance of new combinations and connections?

# Judge

The Judge role is when you evaluate your ideas and decide which ones to implement.

## Be Positive

We tend to confuse negative judgment with evaluation. Most people begin by looking for the things that won't work. In our culture, we are rewarded for "critical" thinking and being able to spot error. Watch the TV game show *Who Wants to Be a Millionaire*, and you will see that contestants tend to approach the multiple choice questions by eliminating the answers they think can't be right. One of their lifelines is having two of the wrong answers taken away.

When you finish a performance, what do you think about? I tend to focus on the few errors I made instead of the majority of things that went right. I'm harder on myself than anyone is. That is true with most entertainers that I've talked with. Doris J. Shallcross said, "We are our own worst critics, extremely hard on ourselves, often dwelling unfairly on the small bit of some effort that went wrong rather than on the big percentage of that effort that went right."

Remember that a principle of synchronicity is that you find what you are looking for, and overlook everything else. That is true in evaluating your ideas. If you start by looking for flaws, that is what you will find. If you start by looking for strengths, that is what you will find. When evaluating ideas, Marshall Cook recommends playing the Angel's Advocate first. Look at everything that is right about the idea, look for hidden potential, and try to think of additional possibilities. Sometimes that process will lead you away from your original idea. That is fine. What you discover may be even better.

I was graduated by California State University Long Beach with a BA in Technical Theater. Herb Camburn or Bill Smith taught many of my design classes. One of the most important things they taught me was how to critique my own work. They said if students relied on them to critique our work, our learning would stop when we left school. If we learned to do it ourselves, we would continue to learn and grow as artists. When projects were due, each student put them on display. A critique session started with the student talking about their own work. The first question our instructors asked was, "What do you like about it?" After I talked about what I felt were the successful elements, they asked, "What alternatives would you try next time?" I wasn't to talk in terms of what was wrong, but in terms of what would make something better. Then after I finished, the other students were invited to make comments. Again, they were to start with identifying successful elements, and then suggest alternatives. Frequently, I was surprised that other students felt some elements of a design were more successful than I did. Finally, the instructor made their comments.

I still try to follow that format when evaluating my own ideas and performances. I have better success doing that with ideas than I do a performance. I also follow that format when coaching an Open Mike session or Red Nose Festival Competition for clowns. I start by commenting on the positive aspects, and then offer alternatives that might be better. I try to make it clear that doesn't mean what they did was bad, but that another choice might be more effective.

A new idea, like a seedling, is fragile. It needs to be protected and nourished until it has a chance to grow stronger. Focusing on flaws can quickly crush it. Be careful about revealing it to others too soon. Too often, they are looking for a tree when you have a sapling. They don't see the potential and their reaction may uproot your idea although it could grow into a mighty oak of an idea.

Fritz Freleng, Bob McKimson, and Chuck Jones, the three directors of the Warner Brothers cartoon unit, held what they called Yes Sessions. The director and writer working on a new cartoon would invite the other directors and writers to attend the two-hour session. After their idea was presented, the concept was open for discussion. The only rule was that they could say anything they wanted as long as it was positive. They could comment on the basic idea, suggest additional gags, propose titles, or anything else that was positive and supportive of the cartoon being worked on. Any form of negative comment was banned. If they couldn't say anything positive, they said nothing. If the idea wasn't any good, the director soon realized that from the silence. However, with six creative people unreservedly committed to positively supporting a concept and making it work, they usually found a way. All the comments were recorded. After the session, the director and writer incorporated what they felt were the best ideas into their story. The results of their method of working are cartoons that are considered classic examples of comedy.

Almost every idea has some value or you wouldn't have bothered considering it. Before you discard an idea, look at it carefully for those elements that you might be able to use in another way. The 3M company makes Scotch Tape. One of their scientists was attempting to improve the glue they use on their tape. He came up with a new formula, but it was easily peeled off. He thought his glue was a failure, but asked others in the company if they could think of an application for the glue. Art Fry worked at the company and sang in his church choir. Art was looking for a way to temporarily mark songs in his hymnal. He put some of the new glue on squares of paper and discovered it worked well for his purpose. That evolved into the Post-It Note, one of the company's best-selling products.

## Look for the Best

Taking a positive approach to evaluation does not mean accepting poor ideas. You are looking for the best ideas.

That is one advantage of starting with more than one idea. We judge things by contrast. When you have many ideas you can compare them to each other. Their relative strengths become apparent. In some cases, you can combine the best elements of several ideas. By having many to choose from, you can be confidant that the one you pick will be the best possible.

Remind your Judge that you are looking for the best that you can do right now. It doesn't have to be perfect, just the best at this time. If you wait for an idea to be perfected before you use it, it will never be used. There comes a point where an idea is good enough to be used. George Will said, "The pursuit of perfection often impedes improvement."

A less than perfect routine or idea can still be very entertaining. Also, entertainment is an interaction with an audience. You can't perfect an idea in isolation. You need to interact with audiences in actual performance situations for an idea to evolve. Your audiences will help you discover the strengths and flaws of your idea. Some of the skills you need to perform your routine optimally can only be learned by actually performing it. Sometimes it takes performing a routine repeatedly before it starts to approach its potential.

What ideas have you not put to use yet? If they aren't perfect, are they good enough? How can you put them to use? Is perfection your goal? What can you do to come closer to that goal? Do you forgive yourself when you fail to reach it?

## Reality Check

When I was working as a producing clown in circuses, I learned to think big and then do a reality check. I started with what a routine would be like if I had a talented cast, unlimited budget, adequate rehearsal time, and plenty of prop storage. Then I began to investigate what was available and practical. Sometimes I would have to find less expensive alternatives. Other times I had to consolidate my props, use only those that were absolutely necessary, and figure out how to fit the remaining ones into the smallest possible space. In some cases I had to make adjustments because the clowns hired by the show weren't capable of doing certain bits of business. However, it is easier to dream big and scale it back then to start with a little idea and try to expand upon it.

I still write the ideal routine and then do a reality check. When I wrote my spotlight routine, I combined spotlight gags used by many different performers throughout history. It has the most complicated light and sound cues of any routine I've created to date. One segment requires precise timing between the spotlight operator and me. That segment also has some magic effects that are not part of any of my other routines. When I was preparing to perform it for the first time, I knew that rehearsal time would be limited. Rather than attempt the entire routine and not be able to do any of it right, I eliminated the most difficult section of the routine. I concentrated on perfecting the portion of the routine that would be possible under the existing performance conditions. It turned out well. The second time that I performed the routine; I performed the same segment, and had some difficulties. I will not add the deleted section until I have mastered the part that is currently in my repertoire.

## Safety Check

One important aspect to consider when evaluating performance ideas is safety, both for yourself and your audience. Here are some things to consider.

Before you do anything, make sure that you have enough room. I saw a clown doing a Whip Cracker routine on a banquet stage with the audience seated on three sides. He was using a long bullwhip without enough room. The people behind him were frightened of the whip, and they moved back as far as the banquet tables allowed. Twice people ducked when he almost hit them with the backlash. Those people certainly did not enjoy his performance. If he had hurt anyone, he would have been liable for their injuries.

Water can make a floor slippery. Baby powder is an even greater hazard for slipping. If you are going to use either on stage, make sure you include provisions for cleaning them up, especially if audience members or other performers will be coming onto the stage later.

Before you use any type of pyrotechnics be sure you have been properly trained and include proper safety precautions as part of your routine. Whenever I juggled with fire torches, I made sure there was a wet towel nearby to quickly smother any flames accidentally set. Fortunately, it was never needed, but I always took that precaution. Venues are increasingly banning the use of fire. In recent years, liability insurance programs for entertainers have been excluding the use of fire.

Terry Davolt warns that at the very least clowns should wear an earplug when using pyrotechnics. Terry wears a hearing aid due to hearing loss in one ear that he partly attributes to handling the pyrotechnics inside the Clown Firehouse with the Ringling Bros Barnum & Bailey Circus™ in 1984. (He said being a sheet metal apprentice for four years before joining the circus is also a contributing factor.) According to Terry, "I was lucky that my father gave me some ear protection muffs like the guys wear at a shooting range. I would put them on right before I caught the prop stick of dynamite being thrown inside the firehouse. Then I'd shoot the twelve-gauge sawed-off shotgun about twenty-seven inches from my right ear. Even with ear protection you can't shoot a shotgun off two feet from your ear twice a day, three times on Saturday, all year long, (a total of 550 shows), and not have some hearing damage. In the telephone pole gag I did with Tom Parish, the squib would blow up about a foot from my ear. So there's another 550 explosions, and I didn't use any ear protection during that gag."

While one explosion may not seem bad, the damage is cumulative and you can develop problems over time without noticing it.

Terry also advises wearing safety goggles when loading squibs, flashpots, or other explosive devices in case of premature detonation. Twice in one week, a squib in a prop went off when he was setting it. He got some powder flakes in his eyes, but no permanent damage. Terry said, "I'll admit safety glasses are a pain in the rear to have to wear just to clip a couple of wires together. But I'm also the first to admit that it is only by the grace of God that I'm not walking around half blind from a couple of direct hits to my face and eyes from the unexpected premature explosions."

## Letting Others Judge

It is wise to listen to the opinion of others, but don't let them usurp your position as judge. Ultimately you have to be the judge of what is best for you.

When Randy Pryor was my juggling coach, I came to value his opinion highly. I was playing around with a ring and two balls and attempting some tricks where the balls passed through the center of the ring. Randy told me the audience would never believe it was happening, and I stopped practicing it. A couple of years later I was playing around with the concept again, and Randy said, "That is too cool. You have got to perfect that." I haven't perfected it yet, but that isn't Randy's fault. I am the one who was responsible for the decision to not pursue the idea.

People's opinions will change. I presented critiques two years in a row at a clown convention. One man told me that the thing I commented on most favorably the second year was something I didn't like the first year. I told him it just took me a year to get used to the idea.

Randy told his students to develop an elephant's hide when listening to the opinion of others. You have to take everything in without letting it penetrate to your heart. Then decide what is helpful and forget the rest.

## Competition Judges

Carole and I entered our Levitation routine in a clown competition because some people wanted to see it, and there were no other performance opportunities at that convention. One judge scored us highly and wrote that it was refreshing seeing people enjoy themselves so much on stage. Another judge marked us down and wrote that we were having too much fun for the characters we were portraying. Obviously both judges could not be right. They were just expressing their opinions. Judges often disagree, yet some entertainers give comments by judges more credibility than those that are made by anyone else. I know some clowns who made drastic changes based on a comment by one judge. Most often, the change resulted in stifling their own creativity.

Alfie Kohn has compiled all the research that has been done into competition. He said, "Competition leads to conformity." This can be seen in variety arts. I was recently in a variety show that opened and closed with acts by magicians who had won major awards. Afterwards, several people commented to me about how similar the two magicians were. Both of them produced doves, vanished a cage full of the birds, performed card manipulations, and did a routine with candles. They even used many of the same verbal jokes.

Frequently in a figure skating competition, somebody will skate to "Carmen" in the woman's competition, dance competition, or pair's competition. At the 1988 Winter Olympics, Katerina Witt and Debbie Thomas both skated to "Carmen." Why? Serious competitors study past winners trying to discover what the judges favor. People who have skated to "Carmen" have done well in past competitions, so skaters continue to use it.

Cal Olson, editor of the *New Calliope*, told me the most requested issue of the magazine is the one containing colored pictures of the makeup competition winners. Those interested in the hobby of competitive clowning scrutinize the pictures looking for clues about what pleases the judges.

Judges tend to reward those things that appeal most to them, which often is that which is most like what they do. At a Clowns Of America International Convention, the top ten winners in the Auguste and Character makeup competitions all used a red, yellow, black, and white color combination for their costumes. The winners in the other three makeup categories used a different color scheme. I checked and discovered that the same panel of judges scored both Auguste and Character, and the majority of the judges used costumes with a red, yellow, black, and white color combination. Different people scored the other categories.

Another reason competition rewards conformity is that there has to be a standard that competitors are judged against. Otherwise, the judges don't have anything to base their opinion on. Often this is specified in the rules, but not always. One of the major clown organizations had a heated debate over whether Whiteface clowns should be allowed to wear colored gloves in competition. Auguste clowns could wear colored gloves, but the rules specified that Whiteface clowns had to wear white gloves. The reason given was that a Whiteface clown supposedly had white skin so the white gloves simulated their white hands. It was pointed out that somebody could wear a colored glove on top of white skin. Also, many of the Whiteface clowns were wearing white costumes making their gestures hard to see because the white gloves tended to blend into the costume when the hands were moved in front of the body. The organization decided to continue restricting the color of gloves for that type of clown to preserve the "purity" of the character. It was many more years before the rule was changed. By then, many Whiteface clowns had already switched to colored gloves in normal performances. I have observed that some directors of competitions and judges tend to be conservative and resistant to change. Changes in the competition rules tend to lag behind changes being accepted by clowns in general.

The standards vary from one competition to another. In one clown competition, those who worked in mime or pantomime were penalized ten points per judge for failing to make "effective use of voice."

Judges admit to awarding conformity. One judge stated that he considered Emmett Kelly to be the original prototype for the tramp clown and evaluated each competitor based on how closely they imitated Emmett.

Some competitions include creativity or originality as an element to be scored. The judges decide what is creative. Six months after Barry DeChant published a skit called Stagecoach in one of his books, a couple performed it in a competition exactly as it was published. They won the competition because the judges gave them the maximum points for originality. Barry said that was just proof that the judges had not read his book yet. Most often, if somebody does something very different, instead of being scored highly for being original, they are marked down in all the other areas for not conforming to that competition's standard. Often they are told that they have violated tradition.

This does not mean that somebody who wins competitions lacks creativity. I know some very creative entertainers who have won competitions. However, it is often through perseverance that they have succeeded. At a time when other figure skaters based their movement on ballet, Elvis Stojko based his upon martial arts. He struggled for many years before judges got used to his different style. He was popular with the public long before he became popular with the judges. The first time I saw Murry compete with his magic act all performed with CDs, he didn't place very highly. A year later, he won first place. Creative entertainers who have won competitions do so because they are also good competitors.

Another reason for not relying on the opinion of competition judges is that some of them base their opinions on false information. The judge who considered Emmett Kelly the first tramp clown was mistaken. The tramp character has existed since 1874, and Emmett Kelly didn't begin performing as a tramp clown until 1933. There is a rich and varied history of tramp clowns from the fifty-nine years prior to Emmett Kelly. That same judge also said tramp clowns shouldn't wear bright colors, but Emmett wore a bright green shirt specifically because he felt his costume needed a bright color to keep it from being too drab. There is a lot of false information about tramp clowns perpetuated by the clown competition system.

According to Alfie Kohn, the only thing competition teaches you to do is be a better competitor. Entering clown skit competitions only teaches you to win clown skit competitions. The format of the competition with short performance periods between set up and tear down breaks does not correspond to actual performances. The nearest it comes to is circus acts, where a minority of clowns perform. Although clown acts in the circus are short, there usually isn't the luxury of having props leisurely set up because the act is used to fill a break in the show caused by props for the other acts being set. Many times, I have seen clowns who have won major skit competition awards fail while attempting to do a show because they have not learned to segue from one routine into another. They would do a skit, and then they would pause to reset their props or they would leave the stage entirely for a costume change. I attended one variety show that was supposed to be thirty minutes long, but it took the clown forty-five minutes to perform four five-minute skits. He had a costume change and a complete change of stage setting and props between each skit. The skits were not dependent upon his costumes, so he could have worn the same costume for all of them. In most cases, he didn't need to change props. He used a white chair in his first skit. Before he started his second skit, he had the prop crew substitute a red chair for the white one. The chair was the same shape and size as the white one, but the red chair matched the red accents in the new costume he had put on.

If you want to learn how to entertain real audiences, you need to look elsewhere for feedback to judge the effectiveness of your material.

## The Audience as Judge

As entertainers, we aren't the final judges of our routines, the audience is.

Randy Munson said, "The only rule is this, did the audience like it?"

Barry Lubin said, "Listen to your audience. They are always right."

According to Fanny Brice, "Your audience gives you everything you need. There is no director who can direct you like an audience."

As entertainers, we want to create a specific audience response. The key to doing that is paying attention to their reactions, finding what they respond to, and adjusting what we do accordingly.

For years, the climax of my act was a four-ball juggling routine. It was the part of my act that I enjoyed the most, and it brought the best audience response. Then I added a combination routine of spinning a plate on a mouthpiece while juggling three clubs. It would frequently bring strong spontaneous applause. The four-ball routine seemed anticlimactic. I tried switching the two routines, but then the plate-club combination didn't receive as good a response as before. The plate-club combination by itself got better response than in any combination with the four-ball routine, so I took out the four-ball routine.

No matter how much you enjoy a routine, its place in your act should depend upon the audience response to it. In general the performance is the time to do things for the audience's enjoyment and rehearsal is the time to do things for your enjoyment. I continued doing my four-ball routine during practice for my own enjoyment and to preserve the skill, which came in handy. In intimate settings, during my three-ball routine, an audience member would sometimes shout, "Do four!" So, I gave the audience what they wanted. It went over very well because the audience knew I was departing from my act to meet a challenge, and I succeed.

Eventually I put my four-ball routine back into my show, just earlier in the act. After juggling three balls, I hold up a sign that says, "Want Me To Juggle With Four?" Then I juggle with two balls and a large numeral four. This draws a big laugh, and then when I actually juggle four balls it gets a big hand.

I believe the advantage a live entertainer has over any other form of entertainment is that they can respond to the audience. Interaction is a key to my performance style. I knew that when I juggled with three balls, somebody would sometimes challenge me to juggle with four. I guessed that when I juggled four balls, somebody might challenge me to juggle with five. So, I prepared a response. I made a large cutout numeral five that I keep in my trunk. If somebody challenges me to juggle with five, I pull out that numeral and juggle it along with two balls. I don't get to use it often. I would guess the opportunity comes up in about 5 percent of my performances. But since it is a reaction to what somebody in the audience has said, the response is always excellent.

Magician Max Maven said he has heard many times that you should let the audience be the judge of your material, but he feels that you can include some things just because you enjoy them.

Milt Josefsberg wrote a joke for Jack Benny's radio program. The joke was, "I think when I get to the TV store, I may buy a new phonograph record. The gang keeps complaining that they're tired of dancing to 'Cohen on the Telephone.'" Jack had four comedy writers at the time. Two of them were Jewish and two were not. The Jewish writers thought the line was great but the others did not understand it. "Cohen on the Telephone," one of the first comedy records, was a routine where Cohen, a man with a thick Yiddish accent, talks to his landlord on the telephone. It had been very popular with Jewish audiences when it was originally released. By the time Josefsberg wrote the joke, the recording was an old one that young people were not familiar with, especially if they were not Jewish. The writers debated deleting the line from the show. According to Josefsberg, "Jack then said a line he often used during these script conferences: 'If we can't devote fifteen seconds in a half-hour program for our own amusement, we're in the wrong business.'"

Jack decided to keep the joke in the script. He said, "Fellows, let's suppose that there never was a record called 'Cohen on the Telephone.' The title sounds funny, and the mere fact that I would have a record called 'Cohen on the Telephone' should get a laugh."

The joke got a nice but not great reaction, from the studio audience. After the broadcast, Jack got a phone call for Cole Porter who wanted him to know how much he enjoyed the reference to the old recording. He thought the joke was hilarious.

Following Jack's example, you can include material for your own enjoyment if it is a small percentage of the overall show and if people who don't understand the background will not realize that they have been excluded from an inside joke. Doing so may increase the overall effectiveness of your show because you perform more joyfully and that joy spreads to the audience.

Because you are concentrating on so many things during a performance, it is sometimes hard to remember audience reactions afterwards. Mike Caveney suggests taking an audio tape recorder with you to record your shows so that you can listen to the audience's reactions.

That is good advice. At a mall appearance, I was using several new routines not part of my regular act. Suddenly a tiny girl seated on her father's lap squealed, "Do it again!" Afterwards, I could not remember which routine had delighted her. Had I recorded that performance, I could have figured out which one it was and definitely would have made it a standard part of my act.

Another technique is to have somebody sit in the audience who can report back comments they have heard. Wild animal trainer Clyde Beatty always used this technique. He then changed his act accordingly. At one point he started using female lions in his act. That made it more dangerous because the males might get into a fight over them. From the comments reported back to him, he discovered people were confused by the addition because they didn't recognize a female lion. Other animal trainers realized the skill required to handle male and female lions, but the audience didn't appreciate it, so he took the females out.

Before a routine becomes too set, try different variations out in front of an audience and listen to their response. They will help you find the best choice.

In one of his stage routines, W. C. Fields answered the phone. He said, "Hello, Elmer . . . Yes, Elmer . . . Is that so, Elmer? . . . Of course, Elmer . . . Good-bye, Elmer . . ." Hanging up the phone, he confided to his wife, "That was Elmer."

According to Fields, "It was a roar. It took ten or twelve performances to find that 'Elmer' is the funniest name for a man. I tried them all—Charley, Clarence, Oscar, Archibald, Luke, and dozens of others—but Elmer was tops."

W. C. Fields was performing his golf routine in the Ziegfield Follies. Although it had nothing to do with the act, Florence Ziegfield decided he wanted one of his showgirls to walk a Russian wolfhound across the stage right in the middle of the routine. Fields was furious at being upstaged, but he decided to take advantage of the situation. When she was halfway across, he commented, "That's a very beautiful horse." According to Fields, "It got a big laugh. I experimented night after night to find out what animal was the funniest. I finally settled upon, 'That's a very beautiful camel.'"

The Marx Brothers would also experiment before a live audience when fine-tuning a routine. For example, when preparing to film *A Night at the Opera*, they performed the stateroom scene as a vaudeville act. They performed it many different ways. By the time they filmed it, they knew what generated the best audience response. The result is one of the most famous scenes in film comedy.

That practice is still done with Broadway shows. Before they have their opening in New York, they schedule performances in other towns specifically to listen to audience response and make changes before they face the New York audiences and critics. Those out-of-town tryouts are an important step in the process of creating a Broadway show. There is less pressure to be perfect so the cast and director feel free to try new approaches. A new musical titled *Hairspray* had their tryout in Seattle a few months before opening on Broadway. They started with a week of preview performances, and asked that theater reviewers delay seeing the show until after the previews. That removed some of the pressure from those first performances giving the director more freedom to try different things during that week.

You should adapt your own version of the tryouts. I use voluntary performances at the Seattle Ronald McDonald House. Carole and I perform there frequently and have made friends with some of the families. I know if a new routine falls flat, I can quickly recover with one of my established reliable routines. Also, they enjoy seeing new things when I return.

When I taught clown classes at Randy Pryor's Southern California School of Magic and Variety Arts (SCSMVA), the last Friday of the month was a variety show for family and friends. The audiences were small and very supportive. If somebody made a mistake and wanted to start over, that was enthusiastically permitted. This provided students a safe atmosphere to try what they had been learning in class. Randy was a friend with many of the leading magicians in the area. They agreed to emcee the shows in return for being able to try out new material. For example, the first performance by Victor and Diamond of their Splitting A Live Rabbit Into Two was at the SCSMVA variety show. That eventually became a very well known effect.

Magician Steve Hart recommends trying something at least three or four times. If you do something only once or twice, the results you experience may be due to unusual circumstances. In the 1960s, when they previewed the pilot episode of the *Batman* TV series, they got the worst audience response they had ever gotten to a preview. According to William Dozier, the show's producer, if the network had not already bought the series it would never made it to the air. When the show premiered in 1966, it was the biggest immediate hit in TV history with a rating share of 55.

Also, the first few times you do something, you won't perform it at your optimum ability. If an idea doesn't work initially, realize that the problem may not be with the idea, but with how you are performing it. Stick with an idea long enough that you begin performing it well. Then you can accurately judge audience reaction.

Sometimes when I have an idea I really believe in, and it isn't getting the response I want, I will take it out of my shows for a while. Then later, sometimes in a year or two, I try it again. An idea that didn't work for me early in my career can be extremely successful at a later stage. Sometimes I have to develop to the next skill level before I am ready to use the idea.

Where can you safely experiment in front of an audience? What shows allow you the freedom to be less than perfect?

Sometimes performers use "audience appeal" as an excuse for not improving their act. They say they can't change something because it gets such great audience response. Getting good response is not always justification for continuing to perform something. When I worked at Raging Waters, I had a large book titled *Jonah*. I opened the book revealing a picture of a whale, and suddenly water would squirt out the whale's spout. It always got a lot of laughs. If I didn't include it in a show, season pass holders would ask me why I had left it out. I could not imagine performing a show without including it. Gradually I realized that while some people laughed a lot when I performed the routine, not everyone laughed. I also came to realize that it interrupted the flow of my show and did not add to the overall impression I was trying to create. I took it out of my shows, and haven't performed it for many years. I believe that the overall response to my show is much stronger without it.

Each time I finally took something out of my shows that I felt got good response, I was able to replace it with something that got better response.

Some performers over estimate the audience appeal of bits of business. For example, a performer will say hello, and when the audience responds, the performer replies, "What was that? I can't hear you." They coerce the audience into shouting hello louder and louder. This technique can be effective when used judiciously. However, just because the audience responds verbally does not mean they were entertained. Duane Laflin refers to this type of opening as "provoking a response before you have earned a response." It can actually work against you. You may get the kids to shout, but alienate the adults sitting next to them. If you use this, you have to read your audience carefully and quit before their interest peaks. If your last response is less than the previous one, you continued it two times too many. I have often seen performers continue this bit past the point of diminishing returns. The audience is no longer shouting louder because they are tired of the game, but as long as the performer is still getting some response, they think the bit is working. I have seen performers completely alienate their audience, and then heard them brag afterwards about what great response they got.

I have also heard performers brag about the response they have gotten when they have simply let the audience get out of control. After the kids have gotten excited, if you can not calm them down enough to do something else they are no longer being entertained by you. If they are doing what they want instead of what you want, they are out of control. They are enjoying their freedom and you are irrelevant. You have no appeal for them if they are not interested in seeing what else you are going to do. It can be fun to get kids so excited that they are bouncing off the walls, but then you have to be able to catch them again and direct their attention to the next routine or activity.

I think some performers overestimate their appeal because they don't know any better. They have not seen a performer get excellent audience response so they don't know what is possible.

How well are people responding to your performance? Are you sure that is an accurate evaluation? Is there something that gets a laugh but detracts from the overall effectiveness of your show? What is getting good response? Is there something you can replace it with that will get a better response?

## Laughter

Jackie Gleason said, "Comedy is the most exacting form of dramatic art because it has an instant critic: laughter."

Everything done by a clown does not have to be funny, but something should. When you identify yourself as a clown, you create the expectation that you will be funny. To be successful as a clown, you should generate laughter from your audience. If you identify yourself as a comedy performer, something must be funny as well.

Do you listen to your critic? Do your routines generate laughter from your audience? Are you a success?

## Is Laughter Enough?

But is laughter enough? Is anything acceptable as long as it gets a laugh?

Laughter does not necessarily mean people are enjoying themselves and being entertained. People laugh for many different reasons. In 1872, Charles Darwin observed that some people laugh during a state of intense pain. Some people laugh when they are embarrassed, nervous, or fearful. The laughter of others may be derisive, sadistic, or contemptuous. Some people will do a phony laugh just because they think laughter is expected. In *Laugh After Laugh*, Dr. Raymond Moody describes physical conditions that cause abnormal laughter. They include pseudobulbar palsy, amyotrophic lateral sclerosis (Lou Gehrig's disease), multiple sclerosis, Wilson's disease, epilepsy, Kuru, poisoning or intoxication by certain chemicals and drugs, Alzheimer's disease, Pick's disease, and Klein-Levin syndrome. Dr. Moody also lists many psychological disorders whose symptoms include abnormal laughter. He said that in some cases the laughter is the first, or only, identifiable symptom providing a clue to what is happening for the person. Laughing at things that you normally would not find funny is a symptom of sleep deprivation.

I saw a magician performing the Twentieth Century Shorts routine. After he tied two scarves together, he tucked them into the waistband of a male volunteer's pants. He said something I didn't hear, and the volunteer, looking very uncomfortable, edged away from him. The magician said, "If he doesn't like me now, he is going to hate me in a moment." The magician proceeded to vanish a third scarf, and then pull on the end of one of the scarves sticking out of the volunteer's pants. There hanging between the two scarves originally tied together was a pair of boxer shorts. The volunteer gave the magician an obvious look of disgust, and the audience roared with laughter. If the magician knew he was going to alienate the volunteer, why did he continue? Not only did the magician alienate the volunteer, but also everyone in the audience who emphasized with him. Remember that an audience volunteer is a proxy for others in the audience and they will feel as if they have been treated the way the volunteer has been. I know that magician has kept that routine in his repertoire so he has continued alienating audience members. Yes, he got laughs, but look at the price he paid. If we abuse audience members in the quest for laughter, is it any wonder that some people dislike magicians, clowns, and other performers? Is it any wonder people look away when performers start selecting volunteers?

Laughter alone isn't enough. I believe that we should set a higher standard for audience response to our performances. Look at what these famous comedians had to say about this subject.

In *Great Comedians Talk*, Larry Wilde wrote, "Maurice Chevalier explained that the comedian's rapport with the audience 'depends on the *quality* of the laugh!' He indicated that a laugh coming out of a warm, human situation is more meaningful and longer lasting than the harsh, quick response that comes from embarrassment or shock. 'You have fellows who make people laugh and at the same time, simply because they laugh, does not mean it is good.'"

According to Milton Berle, "Shock laughter is temporary laughter. It doesn't stick to the funny bone. I don't believe there are 'dirty' words. I do believe there are ugly intentions! In the area of off-color humor, a larger danger exists. Evoked laughter can mitigate against you. An audience may laugh itself sick and hate you as soon as the laughs ebb."

Many entertainers gain laughter at the expense of individuals or specific groups. This is dangerous because you can do real harm with this type of humor. As Leon "Buttons" McBryde said, "Humor is a two edged sword. A lot of jokes are put downs that makes others feel less than human. This type is bad. Don't insult people due to age, race, sex, or religion."

Gene Perret said, "You can never guarantee against offending someone, but comedy is a powerful force and can cause pain if misused. You draw the line on good taste yourself."

If you cause pain with your laughter, you will be resented. My own personal rule is to not use something a person can not easily change about themselves as a subject of a joke. You have to decide for yourself what rule you are going to establish.

Many comedians agree that audience rapport, your relationship with the audience, is more important than laughs themselves.

Jack Benny said, "There has to be something more than just getting laughs. Laughs *are* not everything. People can scream at a comedian and yet can't remember anything afterwards to talk about. To become real successful they must like you very much . . . They must have a feeling like, 'Gee, I wish he was a friend of mine. I wish he was a relative.'"

"If you're a comic you have to be nice. And the audience has to like you," said Fanny Brice. "You have to have a softness about you, because if you do comedy and you are harsh, there is something offensive about it."

According to Woody Allen, "What they (the audience) want is an intimacy with the person. They want to like the person and find the person funny as a human being. The biggest trap comedians fall into is trying to get by on the basis of material. That's just hiding behind jokes."

Jerry Seinfeld said, "If I tell a joke, and they don't laugh, it means that they don't like my joke. It does not mean that they don't like me. If they laughed at my joke it does not mean that I am successful. It means that they liked the joke, not necessarily that they like me."

Steve Smith said, "There is a difference between acting funny and being funny. Don't act funny, be human."

Jimmy Durante asked, "What is the greatest quality a comedian can have? Heart! He's gotta have heart. Without that he's nothing!"

Not just comedians have come to this conclusion. Howard Thurston said, "Long experience has taught me that the crux of my fortunes is whether I can radiate good will towards the audience. There is only one way to do that, and that is to feel it. You can fool the eyes and minds of the audience, but you cannot fool their hearts."

That good will is a powerful tool. I was performing for the second year in a row in the public show at a variety arts conference held in the same town each year. As I entered the auditorium, a woman stopped me. She said, "Oh, good, you are here. You impressed me so much last year, that I brought some of my friends to see you." I quickly began thinking back over the routines I remembered doing the previous year to see which one was so great. I was surprised by what she said next. "As you came in you saw a child whose shoe was untied. You knelt down and tied it for them. You treated them with so much honor." More than the routines I had worked years in developing, she was impressed by my interaction with an individual in the audience.

Bonnie Jean Wasmund said, "People will forget what you said, people will forget what you did, but people will never forget how you made them feel."

According to David Carlyon, "Good clowning is hard because laughs are easy. There will always be someone to giggle if you slap on makeup, throw on mismatched clothes, and make a stupid face. People responded to my makeup and costumes as if I was a clown, but I had gathered enough experience in performing to know that it was because they expected so little from circus clowns. Worst were the polite laughs. They were pity laughs, which meant that those watching believed I was such a bad performer that they had to encourage me. As I learned to clown, my aim matured: I tried to connect."

If your relationship with the audience is so important, how do you build that? One way is with how you treat audience volunteers. Other members of the audience will feel like they have been treated the same way. Look at what you do when you invite a volunteer to join you on stage. What kind of relationship do you have with them? Is that the kind of relationship you want with the rest of the audience? What does that interaction reveal about you as a person? If you were the volunteer, would you like being treated that way?

For me, the eagerness of other people to volunteer for routines later in the show is the best indication of how successful I have been. If I have increasing difficulty convincing people to join me on stage, I know I have done something wrong with a previous volunteer. If I have several willing volunteers to choose from, I know I am on the right track.

Comedy can be a tool in developing a relationship. Studies have shown that if a couple laugh together on their first date, they are more likely to have a second date. The laughter creates a common bond. For an entertainer, especially a magician who is doing amazing feats, one of the most effective types of humor is self-depreciation. That makes the magician more human. During one of his live performance tours, David Copperfield had a stumble going down the stairs choreographed into the performance. After an astonishing illusion, he let the audience see him as somebody capable of mistakes. (The clue that it was planned was that the musical background he uses while looking for an audience volunteer didn't start playing until after the stumble.)

Self-depreciation humor was the secret behind Jack Benny's extremely successful extended career. According to Fred Allen, "Benny was the first comedian in radio to realize that you could get big laughs by ridiculing yourself instead of your stooges. Benny became a fall guy for everybody else on his show."

Laughter is desirable, but it isn't a goal in itself. It is a tool to be used by an entertainer. Like any tool, it can be used to cause destruction or to build something beautiful. A wise entertainer uses laughter to build rapport with the audience and coax them into enjoying themselves. Don't just look at whether people are laughing at your act. Ask yourself, what effect does the laughter have upon them?

## Is It Appropriate?

For humor to be effective, it must be the appropriate material for the appropriate audience at the appropriate time.

For example, at a variety arts conference, jokes about something that has happened earlier in the conference are appropriate for an Open Mike or Demonstration Show. It is usually very effective. Tailoring your material to the specific audience demonstrates that you think they are important. It also gives the performer more credibility by demonstrating their creativity. The shared laughter and recalling something they have all experienced helps to unite a group. A united audience is more responsive because emotions and laughter are contagious. This type of material, unless it is an incidental detail, is not appropriate for a Public Show where a large percentage of the audience did not attend the conference. Inside jokes divide the audience and exclude those who do not know the context for the joke. If a portion of the audience feels excluded often enough during a show, they will become alienated. Not only will they stop responding to the entertainment, but they also prevent crowd dynamics from boosting the response of others.

A type of humor that is definitely not appropriate for every audience is blue humor relying on sexual innuendo and profanity. Some entertainers incorporate that type of humor because they think it makes their act seem hip, modern, or cutting edge. According to Judy Carter, "Comics such as Kinison, Pryor, and Carlin use them (dirty words) to good effect, but more often lazy comics use dirty words because they can't figure out how to make something funny and they think that expletives will help. In many cases unskilled comics will use expletives as a way to camouflage their lack of real passion."

Some venues specifically ban the use of blue material. Disneyland has very strict standards for their live entertainment. At an audition for jugglers, a brother and sister team was standing back-to-back while they passed clubs over their shoulders to each other. The girl said, "Look we are juggling just like Fred Astaire and Ginger Rodgers, cheek-to-cheek." That was enough to disqualify them from consideration.

Even when the venue allows the use of blue material, it still may not be appropriate for all the members of the audience. There may be some people there who find it offensive. Others won't be offended. They just won't find it funny. It is the type of material most likely to receive sympathy laughter. Comedy Clubs have a reputation for accepting blue material, but some managers won't hire somebody using blue material, especially as an opening act, which is the position new comers are placed in. According to Judy Carter, "It sets the tone for the show and makes it difficult for others to follow if they're not in the same blue vein."

Randy Pryor advises that it is best to avoid borderline blue material and use jokes that are appropriate everywhere. That way you don't have to worry about whether or not a joke is appropriate for a specific audience, and you don't risk offending people by making the wrong decision. Also, you can perform your routine the way you rehearsed it without having to edit it during performance. You won't include an inappropriate joke accidentally out of habit.

A local magic club started emphasizing attracting young members as part of preparing the next generation of entertainers. Many teenagers joined the group. Some members were as young as eight years old. Each meeting included an Open Mike session. Some of the older members were accustomed to using risqué material and included it in their performances at the meetings. After repeated complaints from parents, the club started printing a reminder in their newsletter that families attended the meetings and only appropriate material should be used.

One magician told me that he normally works where blue material is acceptable. He tried taking it out when he worked in other venues. He did not have other more appropriate types of comedy prepared that he could substitute, so he simply eliminated the inappropriate humor. Not getting laughs where he was used to them threw him off. His conclusion was to always use his scripted act, whether it was appropriate or not. He said that if somebody was offended, that was their problem, not his. I disagree with him. According to Ronald A. Berk, the negative effects of humor that offends someone are tightening up, withdrawal, resentment, anger, tension, anxiety, and turning off/tuning out. If you offend part of your audience you alienate them and they will not appreciate the other things you do in your act, no matter how good they are.

The effect does not depend upon the amount of inappropriate material in your act. People involved in public speaking are often advised to start with a joke or humorous story to build rapport with their audience. I have heard many people say that when they thought that initial joke was in poor taste, they tuned out the rest of the speech. It did not matter if the rest of the speech was in good taste because the audience was no longer listening.

Early in his career, Jack Benny would use blue material where it was not only accepted but also expected, for example, the Friar's Club. However, Jack learned that somebody had repeated one of his risqué jokes in a setting where women were present, and attributed the joke to Jack. Jack was so upset about that happening, that he immediately made it his policy not to tell any joke that couldn't be safely repeated in any situation.

Jack Benny

Jack Benny considered people's feelings when deciding if material was appropriate. One year, during the summer hiatus from his radio show, he vacationed in England with his wife. After they returned to America, but before the new season started, Shirley May attempted to swim the English Channel. The big news about her attempt was that she did it in the nude to reduce drag. She coated herself with Vaseline to protect her body from the cold water. To start the broadcast for Jack's new season, the writers wrote this exchange between Jack and his announcer Don Wilson:

> Don: Jack, I understand you just got back from England?
> Jack: That's right, Don, I was in England.
> Don: You went there for a vacation, huh?
> Jack: No, I went over to grease up Shirley May.

The joke got a great response at rehearsals, but Jack cut it from the script shortly before the broadcast. He decided that since Shirley May was only seventeen years old the joke might embarrass her or seem to ridicule her. He didn't think getting a laugh was worth possibly doing that to a young girl.

It is not just words that can be inappropriate. Actions can also be inappropriate. I knew a female clown who was hired to distribute helium balloons. She told kids that they had to give her a hug before they could have a balloon. Parents complained to her employer and she was fired for sexual harassment of young children.

In the instructor orientation I was given when I taught clown classes at a community college, I was told that any physical contact done in a way that makes a person feel uncomfortable, including touching their shoulder or holding their hand, can be considered sexual harassment. I am not a lawyer and can not tell you the legal boundaries for sexual harassment. I feel it is better to error on the side of caution than hoping that you know where that boundary is.

I am not saying a clown should avoid hugging children. A hug between a child and a clown can be a special moment. However, my policy is to wait for them to offer me a hug. I never ask for physical contact from them.

There are definite parts of the body that should not be touched. In some of my routines, I cue an audience volunteer to bow by simultaneously pressing on their stomach and tapping their shoulder. I always use a prop like a spinning plate or magic wand to press against their stomach. I never touch the front of a volunteer's body with my hand. Not only do I not touch them, but the props that I use are large enough that people can see my hand and know that I am not touching them. It is not enough to be innocent, but you must be seen to be innocent. When posing for pictures with children or audience volunteers, I always make sure that my hands are visible so somebody looking at the photo can not possibly misinterpret what is happening.

I have been involved in many programs that had a policy prohibiting an adult from being alone in a room with children. Their policy required that there always be two adults present. That was to provide a witness that nothing inappropriate had occurred. I have extended that policy to my performances. I do not do a show without another adult present. That is for my protection. Not only does that prevent false accusations of misconduct, but it also means that I do not have to be responsible for discipline. I require that my clients provide somebody to maintain order allowing me to concentrate on being an entertainer.

Sexual innuendo and profanity are not the only things that can offend people. At the other end of the spectrum, those involved in gospel variety arts ministries should understand that routines considered proselytizing are not always appropriate and may offend some audience members. I have been to many variety arts conferences where the question of Christian ministry routines in public performances has been debated. The conferences schedule instructors to present ministry classes, and when those instructors perform in the public show they naturally want to perform what they do best. However, when a routine with an unexpected religious content is performed there are often complaints either from conference participants or members of the public. A well-respected magician that uses his art as an evangelism tool included a patriotic routine about God and country in his performance in the Gala Show at a magic convention. He tried to be careful to be respectful and not promote any religion. In spite of his intentions, some people were offended and he felt that he needed to write a letter of apology published in the organization's magazine.

According to Brenda "Flower" Marshall, a clown ministry instructor, "Christian clowns may have opportunities to work in some secular settings where the more traditional methods of evangelism would not be accepted. However, every opportunity for clowning may not be an opportunity for Christian clowning. I recently heard a young man on the radio say, 'the right thing at the wrong time is the wrong thing.' If someone has hired you to perform at their event, you become their representative to those in attendance. Any time you are hired for a commercial job (a birthday party or company picnic, etc.) you should not mistake a secular performance for an opportunity to sneak in a gospel presentation. There are times when your faith is better seen and not heard. Don't be so concerned about being 'religious' that you offend instead of entertain. Wearing religious buttons on your costume, handing out religious stickers, or presenting a message verbally, without the permission of your employer, is definitely not appropriate."

A trend in clowning and magic is performing stupid hillbilly bumpkin type characters, and using false buckteeth as the main identifying characteristic for those characters. I had many people comment to me that they found that offensive. Either they had dental problems themselves or they emphasized with those who did. What they objected to was equating dental problems with stupidity. I wrote an article for the *New Calliope* magazine, published by Clowns of America International, stating that I was opposed to the trend. That article got more response than any other single article that I have written. When I attended conferences and conventions, people stopped me to thank me for speaking out and taking a stand. I received many letters from people who appreciated the article. Duane Laflin asked permission to reprint the article in his *Happy Magic* newsletter. In his introduction to the article, Duane wrote, "I have long had the same concerns he does about the so-called Comedy Teeth. To what Bruce writes on the subject, I add my 'AMEN!' I'm grateful that he had the courage to express his point of view and I think we all should carefully ponder what he says."

Some people were vehemently opposed to my opinion about the teeth. They wrote letters to the editor equating using the buck teeth with wearing big shoes or big noses. To me the difference is that in many cases the large nose is in proportion to the other exaggerated facial features and sometimes the big shoes are in proportion to the baggy costumes. Also, the nose and shoes are not used as an identifying characteristic of lack of intelligence. Some performers wear oversized shoes and big noses to play characters that are clever rouges. Is it appropriate to wear buckteeth as the major identifying characteristic of a stupid character? Some people think it is, while others disagree. In the responses that I received, four times the number of people found them offensive than those who thought they were acceptable.

In talking about humor in the classroom, Ronald Berk said, "What is offensive is not determined by a majority vote of the students. It is an individual issue in many cases because humor is open to individual interpretation. However, your experience should weed out most of the offensive material so these individual cases are rare."

As Gene Perret said, you will have to decide yourself where to draw the line on what is appropriate material for you and your audiences. I try to avoid making fun of any physical aspect that people can not easily change about themselves. I try to avoid putting down a member of the audience. I try to avoid sexual innuendo. I try to avoid racial references. I am not always successful, but I try. Where do you draw the line on appropriate material? How do you judge whether you have crossed over the line?

Some types of props may be inappropriate for specific audiences. Because playing cards are associated with gambling and fortune telling, some churches consider routines using cards to be inappropriate.

The schools in the Seattle area have a zero tolerance policy for knives and guns, including squirt guns. They are not allowed on campus. Using any type of weapon in a school show is completely inappropriate in this area. Recently a mother who had booked me for her son's birthday party called me back to ask if I used any guns in my show. When she sent out the invitations, one of her friends said they had been to a birthday party where a magician had used several guns in his show, and they felt that was inappropriate.

Be sure that your material is appropriate to the age of your audience. Poker cards can be inappropriate for young audiences because they don't understand them. Young kids don't know the names of the suits, especially clubs and spades. Bob Keeshan said, "Children are not less intelligent than adults. They just have less experience." When entertaining young children, it may be more appropriate to do magic with cards they are familiar with like Old Maid, Animal Rummy, or Fish. Also, young audiences aren't familiar with the word silks. It is better to call them scarves or handkerchiefs.

Even when your material is appropriate, it may not be the appropriate time. I was working as a clown at a Mexican restaurant, and started to approach two women and an elderly man sitting at a table. One of the women asked me to please leave them alone. I respected their privacy, and entertained other guests who were receptive. As they were leaving, one of the women explained that they were attempting reconciliation with their estranged father and didn't want their conversation to be interrupted.

According to Kenny Ahern, "When you are doing strolling entertainment, you need to be invited into their personal space." I wait until somebody in a group makes eye contact and smiles at me before I approach a group. Then I know they are receptive and it is an appropriate time to entertain them.

During a lecture on impromptu magic, Gregory Wilson said, "You should always be prepared to do magic, but also be ready to not do it." Greg said that when he arrives as a guest at a party, he looks around and decides what he can use in a routine and even makes some preparations. Then if somebody asks him to do something magical, he is set. However, if the appropriate moment doesn't come up, he doesn't push himself upon people.

Many clown instructors teach that you should never drop your character, but being in character is not always appropriate. When I am doing strolling entertainment, and a mother asks me where the restroom is, she is not interested in a comedy routine. She wants me to tell her as clearly as possible how to get to the nearest restroom. Her very real needs are more important than my need to maintain my fantasy character.

People who use a clown character voice need to learn when it is appropriate. When you are backstage, other performers don't want to be entertained and they aren't impressed by your ability to maintain a voice. Backstage they want to relate to you as a person, and want you to respect them enough to relate to them in the same way. Clown makeup and costume is not your character. Just because you look like a clown does not mean you have to act and sound like one. Somebody who insists on using a character voice when it is not appropriate can be very annoying.

Clowns who have chosen a silent character also need to learn when it is not appropriate. Young children may be frightened by the silence because they have never experienced somebody who doesn't speak. I found that a sign of this is that the child will increase their volume as they repeatedly say hello. They are trying to get the person to speak. When I am playing a silent character, and realize this is happening, I kneel down, speak to them quietly to reassure them, and then switch back to my silent character.

Discipline problems are another time when it is appropriate to break character. I've noticed that when a clown, using a silly character voice or motions, tries to reprimand a child for unacceptable behavior, the child thinks their actions are okay because the clown still seems to be playing with them. Speaking in a normal voice lets them know that you are serious. Letting a child disrupt your performance because you don't want to break character only prevents you from being able to entertain the other people as well.

The field of Caring Clowning, entertaining in hospitals and nursing homes, is another place where you need to be sensitive to what is appropriate at that time. Some times the patient or resident may need and welcome the gift of laughter. Other times they want somebody to listen while they talk. A Caring Clown also has to be sensitive to the needs of the doctors and staff. Some of the time they may welcome humor to relieve the stress of their job. At other times, they are busy with something important and being interrupted will only increase their stress level.

How do you decide when it is the appropriate time to entertain? Are you aware of how people are reacting to you? How are you sensitive to the needs of other people?

## Is It Right?

Sam Maloof makes artistic furniture by hand. He said, "I always try to adhere to what I think is right, and that to me, is the most important part of creative work. Fashion comes and goes, but my pieces have to have the integrity of my vision."

Scott Hamilton said, "Integrity and perseverance pay off. The longest distance between two points is a short cut."

That was literally true for me one time. After the show, the client started to hand me some cash. He said, "Let's see, that was $—." The amount he named was five dollars more than we had agreed upon. When I corrected him, he paused, pulled out his wallet, and added another ten dollars.

People who cut corners ethically eventually get caught. I served two terms as World Clown Association Education Director. During my second term, a woman sent me her resume asking that I book her as an instructor at our international convention. One of the credits she listed on her resume was instructing the previous year at the WCA convention. Since I had scheduled the instructors for that convention, I knew she had not taught any classes there. It did not take me long to spot several other false claims on her resume. People involved in planning other conventions and workshops called me asking for my opinion of the class she had taught at the WCA convention and I told them the truth. Falsifying her resume eliminated her from consideration for positions she might have otherwise been offered.

A woman, who was new to clowning, thought she had a creative idea for increasing her bookings. She called other clowns in her area and booked them for appearances on major holidays at fictitious addresses. She thought that would eliminate some of her competition for jobs on those days, and hoped the other clowns might refer some business to her if they thought they were not available. It did not take the other clowns long to figure out what was happening and who was responsible. The idea had the opposite of the intended effect. She alienated the people who might have referred jobs to her so she ended up with fewer bookings.

In college, I took a course titled Mental Hygiene. It was a psychology course required for those with a teaching major. I don't remember the name of the instructor, but I have never forgotten something that she taught. She said, "You are no better a teacher, or anything else, than you are a person." I agree with her that you are no better an entertainer than you are a person.

Carol Fassi was a figure skating coach who guided many champions, including Peggy Fleming and Dorothy Hamill. In *The Encyclopedia of Figure Skating*, John Malone wrote "Also widely admired for his ability to encourage off-the-ice friendships between his students who were in direct competition with one another on the ice, Fassi was a molder of character, not just of technique. Most major coaches insist that character is just as much a part of the ability to win championships as talent is."

Movie Director Ron Howard said, "Directors say a lot about themselves through choices. I don't choose (a film project) unless there is something about it that I find involving and morally defensible. As a filmmaker I've got to be accountable. But it can't be legislated. So I ask myself, 'Am I helping or hurting?'"

Some variety arts organizations have a code of ethics. They tend to be written in general terms that do not help for specific circumstances. You have to decide for yourself the right thing to do in each situation. The code of ethics of the major clown organizations prohibits drinking alcohol while in costume and makeup. At a weekend clown workshop a lively discussion began when somebody asked if that meant you should not work where alcohol was served because somebody seeing you leave might assume you had been drinking. Another clown organization debated whether they should allow a beer company to sponsor their convention, especially since many of the members performed drug abuse prevention programs that included alcohol as an abused drug. Another group of clowns debated performing in the family fun area at a horse race track. Some members felt that it promoted gambling while others felt their entertainment provided a wholesome alternative to gambling.

Making a decision on such issues is part of being a creative entertainer.

How are you accountable? How is your character reflected in the choices you make as an entertainer? How is your integrity reflected in your business decisions and material?

## Does it Fit?

A diamond has to be cut before it will sparkle. The material that is eliminated is not necessarily of inferior quality from the material that is left. It just kept the diamond from being the ideal shape. Routines also need to be cut to the desired shape before they sparkle and shine. You may have a wonderful idea when considered independently. However, it may not fit into a routine. It may interrupt the flow or slow the pace. It may break the mood that you are creating. It may distract the audience from something that is more important. It has been said that the good is the enemy of the best. People are often reluctant to remove good material from their acts, but if they would, they will discover that their act is better. Comedians are often advised to create a five-minute routine by writing a ten-minute routine and then cutting half of it out as they perform for audiences and discover what gets the best response.

## Is it an Improvement?

A magician I know was telling me how disappointed he is in the number of magicians who perform the Half Dyed Hank routine using red and white scarves because that is the only color combination commercially available. He feels this demonstrates a lack of creativity. So, he dyes his own silks so he can do it with a different combination, for example yellow and green. It is different, but it is not any better than the original. Creativity is a new response that meets a need.

Audiences aren't interested in the color of the scarves, they just notice that it is changed half way.

In some cases, using a scarf that is a different color just for the sake of being different is less effective. For magicians working on stage, red is actually a good choice since that color is enhanced by normal stage lighting which is designed to flatter flesh tones. In my own routines, I use a red and yellow color scheme a lot, so the red scarf fits what I do. As an introduction, I sometimes use a routine where a red scarf turns into a black sock. I purchased the effect commercially, and it came in red. It makes sense to pair that with the red half dyed hank. I have also used the commercially available version in Christmas performances because it was the colors of Santa's clothes.

Using a different color scarf would be creative if the magician used an overall color scheme that the red conflicted with. It would be creative if the performer was using the colors of the scarves to represent something in presenting a message, for example using black and white scarves to represent the Yin Yang as you explain that opposites often need to be kept in balance.

I do a silk magic routine where I produce three scarves. Each has a picture of one of the three main types of clown characters. After I produce each one, I use it in some other magic effect. I take the Auguste clown on a yellow background silk, push it through my hand, and it turns solid blue. I start to push the blue silk back through my hand and it begins changing back to the yellow silk with a clown face on it. I stop half way, and open my hand. The silk is now half-blue and half-yellow with half of a clown face. I think that is an improvement because I changed the silks to fit into an act that is tied together by a theme. Also, I think using the picture silk makes the half-and-half silk look more interesting and therefore more entertaining.

Is your idea really an improvement? What value is there in doing it a different way?

## Intuition

Sometimes entertainers make a decision without being sure of the reason. They just have a feeling that it is right. That is referred to as intuition. Some people believe intuition is a mystical force outside of yourself that will tell you what is right if you tune into it. I believe that it comes from right-mode thinking making connections with your previous experience. You aren't aware of the memories that match up with the new experience to create that feeling of rightness. To develop your intuition about performing requires experience as a performer.

Tommy Wonder said, "One of the best ways I know of to polish the talent one has is to use it as much as possible. In other words, practice and perform magic as much as you can. In doing so, you will come to see and feel almost automatically how you should do things: you will sense when it is right . . . Before you can hope that intuition will lead you to correct decisions, it is first necessary to develop it as much as you can. The intuition, the feeling, must be developed by intensive practice and performance. If you fail to achieve this development, basing decisions on intuition will be an incorrect approach. One can't base decisions on a sense one does not yet possess."

*"Trust your hunches. They are usually based on facts filed away just below the conscious level."—Dr. Joyce Brothers*

*"We've learned from experience that truth will out."—Richard Feynman*

# Warrior

The Warrior role is the one where you turn your ideas into reality. In many ways, this is the most important role in the creative process. A person who has mediocre ideas that they actually use is more creative than the person is who has tremendous ideas that they have never used. There is no value in having ideas if they are not put into action. The worst idea that you have used is better then the greatest idea that you have never used. You don't get credit for your intentions, only for your accomplishments.

Sometimes people don't put their ideas into action because they don't think the idea is good enough. They are looking for oak trees, and ignore the saplings they have available. Take a small idea, and act on it. A simple little routine may eventually grow into a wonderful act.

By putting a small idea into action, you will learn things about the creative process and about yourself that will make it easier to put great ideas into action.

## Set a Deadline

Often we have ideas for something we want to do someday. However, someday never comes. Many people find that setting a deadline to accomplish something helps them get started. Instead of being a vague desire, it becomes a definite goal.

Some people need the pressure of an impending deadline to motivate them. They will stay up late trying to get something done just in time. I tend to work better when

I am a little more relaxed. I want the opportunity to take time off to pursue other interests. I try to estimate how long it will take. Then I double that since I have learned everything takes longer then you expect. That gives me a date to start working on the project.

I know several magicians who come up with the idea for a show, but do not actually begin writing and building it until they have booked the first performance. That show then gives them a deadline to have the show completed. Some of them say they need that pressure to motivate them to get the show finished. Others say they don't want to spend a lot of time developing a show if they are not going to have a market for it.

## Break It Down

I didn't write this book all at once. I broke it down into chapters and sections. Then I worked on each chapter separately. Finishing each chapter gave me a feeling of accomplishment. Doing it any other way would have been overwhelming.

Our home is surrounded by trees. After a windstorm the cleanup needing to be done can seem overwhelming. I look at the damage and instead of thinking about the entire project; I decide the first thing that needs to be done. I do that. When I am done I decide on the next step. I keep doing things one step at a time as long as I have energy. I tell myself that I don't have to do everything the first day and often I leave something for another time. However, I frequently surprise myself and quickly complete what at first seemed like an impossible task.

You don't have to know how you are going to complete a project. You just have to decide on the first step and complete that.

Martin Luther King Jr. said, "You don't have to see the whole staircase, just take the first step."

Gene C. McKinney said, "If you go as far as you can see and then get there, you'll be able to see a little bit further and go on."

What idea do you have that seems like a big project? How can you break it down into a series of smaller projects? What is the first thing that needs to be done? How can you accomplish that?

## Become an Expert

When you are looking for new ideas in the Artist role you try to maintain the fresh perspective of the beginner. However, for the Warrior role you need to call upon the knowledge of an expert.

Before you have the skill and knowledge to make your ideas a reality you have to master the fundamentals. Amateurs have been able to produce some fresh interesting things that succeed because their enthusiasm overshadows their flaws. However, enthusiasm will only take you so far. Consistently producing the best results requires mastering your craft. According to the Bible, "It is not good to have zeal without knowledge, nor to be hasty and miss the way." (Proverbs 19:2, NIV)

Best selling mystery writer Mary Higgins Clark tells writers, "I think it's wise to somehow be connected to the community of writing. I tell beginning writers, 'Take a course.' It's not just having the talent, you have to learn the craft."

One of the fastest growing specialties in clowning is Caring Clowning, working in hospitals and nursing homes. This type of performance is also known as Therapeutic Humor. Richard Snowberg tells Caring Clowns, "All your props are tools which can be used for a specific strategy. When a carpenter goes into a home to do some remodeling, he doesn't always know which tools he's going to need. From experience he expects a great variety of situations, so he comes equipped with a large toolbox. The more professional a carpenter becomes the more he can do with his tools. The same can be said about a caring clown. You need to have three things: 1) A variety of tools/props, routines, or strategies with which to work, 2) The skill to get the most out of your tools, and 3) the ability to determine which tools to use."

I did a birthday party for a five-year-old boy whose mother said he was very shy. This was going to be his first party of any kind. She asked me to be careful not to overwhelm the kids when I came in. I came in slowly, gave the kids a chance to see me, and shook a few hands before I turned on my music and started my show. It turned out that all the guests were shy as well. I discovered very quickly that my audience interaction routines were not going to work because I could not get much verbal response from the kids. I could not get the kids to leave their seats to assist me with my routines. So, I would hand somebody a magic wand and let them tap a prop from where they were sitting. I changed my presentations to give kids as many opportunities as possible to tap something with the wand. If I dropped a juggling prop, I had somebody tap it with the wand so it would work right. I have a plastic bird that is counterweighted so it will balance on its bill. I got it out and let each of the kids balance it on their finger. I got out a coin, and went down the line vanishing the coin and reproducing it from behind each child's ear. I could not get one little girl to participate. She refused to hold the bird. When the coin vanished, she leaned back away from me so I reproduced the coin from under the paper plate sitting on the table in front of her. I always offered to let her do what the other kids were doing and respected her decision not to participate. At the end of the party, I posed for a group photo with all of the kids. This little girl ended up standing next to me. I put my hat on the birthday boy's head for the picture. She immediately took the hat off his head, and gave it back to me. That was our first direct interaction. When the hostess announced that it was time for me to leave, this little girl ran up and gave me a hug.

The next weekend, I was part of a circus-themed banquet and ball. One of the group's members had a dog that could do tricks, and I was informed that she would do her dog act just before my juggling act. Most of the people could not see the dog performing on the floor between some tables. The dog didn't do much anyway. The emcee kept trying to ease her off the stage, but she kept saying, "Oh, no, we have one more trick." By the time her act was over most of the audience was standing around talking. I had the sound man hit my music right away and I came dashing forward to begin my plate spinning routine. I knew I had to be very energetic to grab everyone's attention and demonstrate that I was going to be worth watching. People did sit down and pay attention. I kept the energy level up and held their interest with some interaction routines.

Those two shows required different techniques to make them a success. It took being an expert to know how to adjust my performance to each audience.

Leonardo da Vinci said, "Those who become enamored of the art, without having previously applied to the scientific part of it, may be compared to mariners who put to sea in a ship without rudder or compass and therefore cannot be certain of arriving at the wished for port."

According to Dr. Harlan Tarbell, "Fundamentally, the making of a magician is no different than the making of other professional people. One must be trained in the mechanics, the alternate methods and be skilled in the presentation in order to meet any conditions which may arise. Genius makes his work a science as well as an art. He has to have basic fundamentals well in mind in order to know where to individualize or exaggerate. Even the cartoonist with his funny caricatures has to learn to draw the human figure in its correct proportions. Knowledge leads to greater heights."

At the Walt Disney studio, William Cottrell served an apprenticeship as an inker, painter, cameraman, and cutter before he joined the story department. He said that technical training was very helpful because, "I knew how to do it mechanically . . . it could give you ideas of how to accomplish something that you wouldn't think of doing before without that knowledge."

The craft of entertainment includes how to set up a joke, act structure, timing, establishing audience rapport, working with audience volunteers, pacing, building to a climax, controlling focus, movement, creating your own material, and so much more.

How much do you know about your chosen entertainment specialty? How much of an expert are you? Where are there gaps in your knowledge and skills? How can you become even more of an expert? Where can you obtain additional knowledge?

## It Takes Work

It is fun to generate ideas. That is play. Completing the process and turning those ideas into reality is work. Animation director Chuck Jones grew up near Charlie Chaplin's Hollywood Studio. Jones said, "My father came home to tell us that he had seen Chaplin shoot a single fifteen-second scene 132 times. It was the beginning of my understanding of the two primary rules of all creativity. The first is that you must love what you are doing; the second is that you must be willing to do the often dull and tiring work necessary to bring each creative endeavor to completion, and in that endeavor only the love should show. It took Chaplin more than a hundred takes a thousand times to bring his incredible craft to the screen he loved so well, and never, never did the work show."

In Chaplin's film *City Lights*, a blind Flower Girl sold the Little Tramp a flower thinking he was a wealthy tycoon. Chaplin filmed that scene 342 times before he was satisfied with it.

Charlie Chaplin

Randy Pryor kept reminding his juggling students that it takes work. The only way to learn to do a juggling trick is to put in the time and effort practicing it. You never will master a trick if you quit because you fail on your first attempt. Randy also advised his juggling and magic students to not be afraid of a trick that took practice to learn. Tricks that require effort to learn have several advantages. First, if it were easy, everyone else would copy you. Second, once you have mastered a trick, you have it. You don't have to keep relearning it. It is like riding a bike. It takes a struggle to learn how to do it, but once you know it becomes easy. If you don't ride a bike for a while, you may be out of shape and not able to ride very long, but you have not forgotten how. Third, when you succeed you take pride in your accomplishment that translates into stage presence.

Julie Dannenbaum, American Chef, said, "The best way to learn to cook is to cook: Stand yourself in front of the stove and start right in."

You can attend classes, read publications, and study videos, but the only real way to learn something is by doing it. You can't learn to juggle without picking up some props and doing it. The best way to learn to use a Thumb Tip is to get one and start using it. The best way to learn to become a clown is by actually performing as a clown. You have to do the work yourself.

It is not just mastering a physical skill that takes work. To build a prop requires setting aside the time, obtaining the materials, and getting out the right tools. If it is different from any prop that you have built before, you may encounter unexpected problems and frustrations.

Be patient with yourself. Give yourself permission to take time to accomplish your goals. Things that grow quickly and easily are the weakest. A mushroom grows overnight while an oak tree grows over many years.

Dean Keith Simonton, psychology professor at the University of California, Davis, said, "Greatness is built upon tremendous amounts of study, practice, and devotion . . . For most of us it's not that we don't have the ability, it's that we don't devote the time. You have to put in the effort and put up with all the frustrations and obstacles."

According to Henry David Thoreau, "If you have built castles in the air, your work need not be lost; that is where they should be. Now put foundations under them."

Many years ago, I put up a storage shed in the backyard of my parent's house. The hardest part was making the foundation. I dug out a hole where the foundation would be, built a wooden frame, lugged bags of concrete mix, mixed the concrete and water by hand, moved the concrete using a wheelbarrow, and poured the concrete. Because it has a solid foundation, that shed is still standing. Putting a foundation under your dream castle is hard work. But it is important to keep it from collapsing.

The first time that I performed a solo stage show in a small local theater, my wife commented that she knew it was a dream come true. It had been a long-term goal of mine. I was very satisfied with how the show turned out. Its success was the result of the foundation I had laid. I had built the backdrop for the set eight years previously. I built one of the set pieces twenty years earlier. The show was on a thrust stage so I used my experience from working in circuses over twenty years ago to play to the audience on all three sides being sure no section got left out. I used some routines from my circus acts. I used some routines from the stage shows I performed during my eleven years at Raging Waters. I used my experience performing on stage at variety arts conferences during the past fifteen years. I have continued my education, and some of the routines that I used were based on things I learned from classes the previous year at magic workshops.

While I was creating the show, I had been doing what I knew to try to book it. I sent out promotional material. I auditioned for arts commissions. Sometimes I failed the audition and sometimes I was placed on their list of available shows. I did platform shows for park and recreation departments. I did stage shows that were part of arts festivals. At times, I met with more success than at others but I kept plugging away. Finally, the work paid off.

What dreams do you have? What can you do to turn that into a reality? What foundation does your castle in the air need? What skills do you need to learn? How can you continue your education? How can you gain experience that will help with your dream? What things do you need to make that will be part of the physical structure of your castle? It is fun to dream, but it takes work to turn that into reality. What can you start working on now?

How much do you love being an entertainer? Do you love it enough to put in the work necessary to get the results you want? How much effort are you willing to expend on being an entertainer? Are you willing to do the repetitious work necessary to make it seem easy and graceful? When you are working on creating a routine, how can you keep in mind the final result and let that motivate you when the practice is less than enjoyable?

## Confidence

George Lucas said, "You can't do it unless you can imagine it. You can't do it unless you can imagine yourself succeeding at it."

If you don't think you will succeed, you will be reluctant to begin. If you think that you can do it, you will keep working until you do succeed.

Frustration is often part of the creative process. You need confidence to carry you through that period of frustration. Early in my career as a clown I found a plastic two-foot long cannon in a thrift store. It had been designed to fire lightweight plastic balls, but they were missing. It had a spring inside that propelled the balls. There was a metal rod extending up the middle of the barrel to guide the balls. I bought it because I wanted to rig it so a flower would pop out of the end of the barrel. I decided to attach the stem of the flower to a tube that would slide up and down the rod. I put a fishing line leash on the tube to stop it when it reached the end of the barrel. I thought it was going to be a simple process, but I was wrong. First, the leash got in the way of the firing mechanism so it wouldn't release. Then the leash got tangled and stopped the flower before it appeared. I got those problems fixed, and still it wouldn't work right consistently. I knew it should work, but it didn't, and I could not figure out why. I kept making adjustments. I knew I was smart and should be able to make it work. After six hours one day, and five hours the next, I was about ready to give up. Then it started to work. I never did find out what the problem was. If I hadn't been confident in my ability, I would not have persevered long enough to experience success. I used the cannon successfully in several parades. Audiences seemed to like it.

Confidence comes from experience. I thought I could get the little cannon to work because earlier in my life I had made other things work. I relied on the memory of the little plastic cannon while working on another cannon prop. I created my Chicken Cannon routine for a pirate themed show at Raging Waters. I thought using pyrotechnics in the cannon was impractical. I decided to create a variation of the bang gun inspired by an episode of the *F-Troop* television show that I remembered. In that show, the Indians fired cannons and "Boom" banners popped out. I decided to use an appearing cane as the flagpole for the banner. Remembering the problems I had with the little cannon, and that it might take longer than expected, I started working on the boom banner a month before my deadline. I started with a plastic appearing cane, which wasn't strong enough. I switched to a metal appearing cane. It still wouldn't work right. I asked all the magicians I knew for suggestions. They all agreed that it should work, but couldn't suggest any possible solutions. The Chicken Cannon routine was going to be a major part of my show, so I couldn't give up. I remembered that with the flower cannon I had to keep making little adjustments. I kept trying with the new cannon. I tried different ways of folding the banner. I tried different ways of holding the banner before it was produced. I adjusted the supports for the cane. Some days I couldn't look at the cannon due to frustration. I had to go do something else or I would take a hammer to it. Finally, about ten o'clock the night before the show was to premiere, I got it to work. Again, I don't know what had caused the problems I was having. I just know that eventually I tinkered enough that I got the right combination for success.

How do you handle frustration when you have difficulty getting something to work? When have you persevered long enough to succeed despite frustration? What helped you keep going? How can you use those experiences to help you deal with future frustration?

One way to boost your confidence is to start an encouragement file. This contains anything that confirms your abilities. That may include letters from satisfied customers, reviews of your performances, newspaper or magazine articles that mention you, and motivational quotes. When somebody makes a comment to you after a show, write it down and add it to your file. Then when you begin to doubt yourself, read the file as a reminder that you have succeeded in the past so you can succeed again in the future.

Confidence that you can do it can provide the motivation to work on making it come true. John Kao said, "Belief also begets discipline. Weekend musicians can belt out some sweet tunes, but the greats practice every day. If you are satisfied with mediocrity, hey, feel free to have a creative burst now and then before quickly settling back into a deadening routine."

The entertainers who achieve greatness believe they are capable of that. Then they work to make it happen. They maintain a practice schedule. They develop their skills. Instead of waiting for inspiration to strike, they work at creating new material. They continue their education, and apply what they learn.

According to Steve Smith, "There is a difference between confidence and cockiness. We want to be confident."

Mike Martz, Head Coach of the St. Louis Rams, said, "You get used to a certain level of success and you take it for granted. You forget how hard you worked to get there."

After a decade of clowning, I briefly became a circus producer. Ed Russell, my partner, and I produced Spot Dates, which means we would sign a contract to provide a client with a circus for a specific date and hire acts for that particular time and spot. We had a one-day contract for two performances. The Ringmaster we liked to use was not available, so we hired an entertainer to do a magic act, emcee the show, and handle the cassette tapes of music for the acts. He was an accomplished magician, but this was his first experience as an emcee. He was very nervous before the first show. He kept double checking that he had the cassette tapes in the proper order and kept rereading his announcement cards. His performance was flawless. He decided that being an emcee was easy, and he relaxed between shows. The second performance was a disaster. Sometimes he put in the wrong music tape or put the right one in backwards. The announcement cards had gotten out of order so he introduced some acts at the wrong time or improvised an introduction that was inappropriate for the act. He had not realized that the first performance was easy because of his thorough preparation. So, he did not prepare as well for the second performance, which made it extremely difficult. He learned his lesson that day, and has become a very successful circus illusionist and ringmaster.

I wish I had learned the lesson along with him. There have been times when one of my performances or classes was less successful than I would have liked because I took my previous success for granted and did not prepare as well as I should have. My best performances have been those where I made an extra effort during the preparation phase.

How successful are your shows? Have you started to take that for granted? Think back to your most successful performances. How hard did you work on those shows? What did you do to prepare? Do you still work that hard on your current shows? Are you less prepared? What can you do to remind yourself to be that prepared?

## Willingness to Risk Failure

Confidence in yourself can give you the freedom to try something new that might fail.

The reason many people do not turn their ideas into reality is fear. Fear of being foolish. Fear of failing. Fear of a dream ending.

A man joined a clown club I belonged to because being a clown was his life long dream. We eventually started calling him the Ghost because in three years he never appeared in a performance. He kept saying he was working on his costume and that it was almost finished. He did not appear as a clown because he did not have confidence that he would succeed. As long as he did not actually perform as a clown, he could still dream about being one. If he did perform, and failed, the dream would be over. For him, the price of failure was too great to risk.

But if you are going to be creative, you will fail sometimes. Some things will be more successful than others, but you will have failures. Randy Pryor kept reminding his juggling students that, "before you can be good, you have to be bad. Before you can be bad, you have to do it." That sounds pessimistic, but I found it encouraging. Failure is just one step in being successful. It was okay to try something and fail, because if I kept going I would eventually succeed. Trying and failing was better than not trying.

Herb Camburn gave his theater design students a lot of options when he assigned projects. He kept asking his students to challenge their abilities and themselves. We would get a better grade for an interesting failure than for a safe success. He knew we would not learn and grow if we kept doing those things that were easy for us to do. We could learn more from a failure if we were able to figure out why it failed, or at least determined a different approach to try the next time.

Something I have heard many times in motivational speeches is, "Consider the turtle, he never gets anywhere without sticking his neck out."

Randy Pryor put it into juggling terms when he said, "If you are not dropping you are not advancing."

According to Dick Buttons, "Every skater knows when you stop falling you stop improving."

Many adults who try ice skating are worried about falling. That fear makes them stand straight and stiff trying to maintain their balance while skating. That rigidity makes it more likely that they will loose their balance. Beginning ice skaters tend to stay close to the boards surrounding the rink, but that causes more falls. Kicking the boards can knock your feet out from under you and trying to hold onto the boards can pull you off balance. To prevent falls skaters need to relax and move further onto the ice. In beginning skating classes the first lesson is often the proper way to fall. When students discover that most falls do not cause pain and falling properly decreases the risk of injury, they are more likely to forget their fear and enjoy skating even when they do fall.

Would you consider somebody who fails over two thirds of the time a success? That is true in baseball. If somebody bats over 300 they are considered a great batter. That statistic means they succeed less than a third of the time. Baseball is a wonderful metaphor for being a creative entertainer. Harold S. Kushner said, "Life is like the baseball season, where even the best team loses at least a third of its games and even the worst team has its days of brilliance."

To me, that is encouraging. I have seen new entertainers do some wonderful things. You can initially have some moments of great success. You won't always fail. It is worth taking a chance because you might succeed. On the other hand, if you are trying to be creative, you will always have failures. No matter how much skill and experience you have, you can never guarantee against failure.

Taking risks, and failing, is part of mastering any skill. Animation director Chuck Jones said, "I heard a brilliant old teacher named Francois Murphy at Chouinard Art Institute repeat to a shocked beginner class, 'every one of you birds has a hundred thousand bad drawings in you. The sooner you get rid of them, the better it will be for everybody.'"

One way to make risk acceptable is to limit the emotional cost of failure. There is a big difference between doing something in practice and doing it in performance. I know that even if I can do it smoothly in practice, I will probably fumble the first few times that I do it before an audience. I look for low-pressure situations to perform my routines in for the first time. One of the advantages of belonging to a local magic club is that their meetings usually include an Open Mike session. When I was a member of the Orange County Magic Club, creativity was openly encouraged. There were some basic understandings for the Open Mike sessions. Every thing performed was the intellectual property of the entertainer and was not to be copied by other members. Every thing was a work in progress. Mistakes were not only tolerated, but anticipated. No negative comments were made about any performance. This did not mean the club excused actual performances that were sloppy. It was just understood that those things done in Open Mike were not up to performance level and the entertainer was not yet ready for a critique. If a performer had great difficulty with a routine, they could simply stop at any point and sit down. If they wanted to try again later in the evening, that was allowed. When somebody repeated a routine during the same night, they were given a standing ovation in recognition of their courage no matter how well their second attempt turned out.

If performing in front of other entertainers increases the emotional risk for you, look for someplace where it is safe to perform before a small public audience. This is different from testing audience reaction. You are testing your ability to perform the material. Some of the members of the Lynnwood Magic Ring of Fire (IBM Ring 339) have made arrangements with a small shopping center to use their permanent stage in their food court one Monday night a month. There is no charge for the Magic Monday show. Since Monday is the center's slowest night, the audience tends to be small. If somebody makes a mistake, not many people see it.

I mentioned earlier that another place I like to try new material is my voluntary performances at the Seattle Ronald McDonald House. That is where I have performed many of my routines for the first time.

Another approach is to limit the amount of new material in any one show. Liberace advised Siegfried and Roy to change at the most 50 percent of their show at a time. If the majority of the material was reliable routines they could perform well, they were insured of an entertaining show even if some the new material was not as successful as they liked.

Experiments have proven that you remember the beginning and end of something the best. That means the middle of a regular show is a good place to put new material that you are trying out. If it doesn't get the kind of response you want, people won't remember that. If it is a new juggling trick, and you drop, people won't remember that either.

Limiting the financial cost of failure can make risk more acceptable. I was on the costume crew for several productions in college. Sometimes we were creating shapes, like dragon tails, that we had no experience with and for which there were no patterns. So, whenever somebody drafted a pattern, we first cut it out of inexpensive unbleached cotton muslin. We sewed it together, and the performer tried it on. Errors weren't important because they could be corrected by cutting and pinning or by stitching on some extra fabric. That would not show in the final product. When we were sure we had it right, we used the muslin pieces as our pattern to cut the more expensive fabrics. If the costume needed to be lined, we could then use the muslin pieces as the lining.

The muslin pattern was our prototype, a version made with less expensive materials or those that are easier to work with. Prototypes are often made for large magic illusions or a prop that will be heavily decorated. Often two prototypes are needed before you are ready to build the final version. The first version reveals the obvious flaws. The second version reveals the important flaws that the obvious ones were hiding.

When Lou Jacobs was developing his famous miniature clown car routine, he built a car out of cardboard. Then he got in, and had somebody mark off the excess space. He built several cardboard mock-ups until he was sure he had the smallest possible design that he could fit into. Then he built an actual working model. On his first attempt to drive it, he discovered he hadn't provided enough vision, and unable to see where he was going, he crashed into a tree. Eventually, he had a car that worked well, and he used it for over forty years.

When Lee Mullally makes a new type of foam prop, especially if it is a custom order, he makes two at the same time. In effect, he makes the prototype simultaneously with the finished product. That way he does not have to remember what he did and repeat it later. If he decides there might be a better way to do something, he immediately tries the alternative method with the other prop. When he is finished, he ships the best version to his customer and either keeps the other for his own use or sells it at his dealer table.

Frankie Saluto and Lou Jacobs

Some performers use the prototype in initial performances to test audience response. Then if it fails, they have not invested as much time and effort in building the prop or illusion. Business leaders refer to this as a quick failure.

Many people fear failure because they consider it a dead end. They view a failure as permanent. A guided missile does not go directly to its target once it is aimed and fired. It frequently gets off course and then is guided back to the route that will take it to its target. During its flight the course of a guided missile has to be corrected many times. In entertainment, a failure is your course correction. It tells you that you need to change your direction to reach your goal.

Over a period of fourteen months, Edison tried sixteen hundred materials as elements in his sealed vacuum incandescent light globes. He said, "Even if you give much time and effort to learning the hundreds of wrong ways of doing a thing, it might lead, in the end, to the right way."

In my college science classes, I learned a principle called successive approximation. You would make a guess, and test to see how close you had become. I think of my performances as successive approximations. They may not be on target yet, but with each show, I try making a small change to see if I can come closer to achieving what I want. That is how I learn the proper timing for a routine. I may realize that I didn't get the response I wanted because I rushed something too much for the audience to appreciate what is happening. So, in the next performance, I try slowing it down a little. Eventually, I discover that I have slowed it down too much and need to pick up the pace a little more.

Some people fear failure because they consider it an all or nothing proposition. They think that if any element fails, the entire thing is a failure.

Some people fear failure because they don't separate themselves from their effort. If they build a prop, and it does not work, they do not think the prop was a failure. They think they are a failure. To them the prop failing is just proof that they are stupid or incompetent.

According to Zig Zigler, "Many people have poor self-image because they set standards of perfection that are unrealistic and unreachable. When they fail—and fail they must—they never forgive themselves. They feel they must either be perfect—the best—or the worst."

The way Duane Laflin expressed it is, "Don't expect perfection. Seek it, strive for it, but don't expect it."

Not expecting perfection allows you to take risks because you realize that something that is not completely successful is not a complete failure either. Not expecting perfection allows you to forgive yourself for making mistakes. I work very hard to develop my technical skill as an entertainer, but I rarely have a technically perfect performance. Sometimes the moves aren't as smooth as I would like. Sometimes I fumble a little with a prop. Sometimes my timing is a little off. Sometimes I forget a bit I intended to include in the show. Often I drop a juggling prop. I am very aware of those mistakes, but the audience rarely notices. Although I failed to do a perfect performance, I still succeeded in entertaining that audience. That is the important thing.

That doesn't mean I advocate accepting mediocrity. Although I know I won't achieve perfection, I realize that striving for it means I will come closer more often.

When you fail, make sure that it is a smart failure. Figure out what caused the failure and how you can prevent that in the future. Failing because you do the same thing you did before hoping to have a different result is not smart.

It is not good to overcome your fear of failure completely. A little fear prevents you from becoming cocky. When fear of failure makes me nervous before a show, I expend that nervous energy by checking my props several times to make sure they are properly set. Sometimes I discover the second or third time I check that I have done something wrong.

Explaining why he discontinued his "Far Side" cartoon, Gary Larsen said, "You need a balance of fear and confidence, and not have one overpower the other. I thought I might lose the fear and start to coast."

How can you make failure acceptable? How can you limit the cost of failure? Where is it safe for you to fail? How can you turn failure into a stepping stone to success?

# Preplan

In my college technical theater classes, I was taught to preplan things using drawings and scale models. Herb Camburn said it is better to make your mistakes on paper. In the drawing stage it is easy to try changes. For example, after drawing a costume design, we might use tracing paper to try different sleeve lengths and widths. We would not draw the entire design again. We would just draw on the tracing paper the part that we considering changing and lay it over the original design.

When we were working on a set design, we would sometimes build a model of the set. In college we used illustration board, but now I might use foam core which is easier to cut. Using the model we could check to make sure the set looked pleasing from different parts of the theater and that nothing was blocking important sight lines. We could also make sure that the proportions were pleasing from each angle.

Once we were satisfied with our design drawings, we would often make construction drawings. We would figure out how something should be built and how the pieces were to fit together.

What kind of planning will insure your success?

# Get Organized

A. A. Milne said, "Organizing is what you do before you do something, so that when you do it, it's not all mixed up."

For me a performance or class begins long before it is scheduled to begin. It begins during the preparation period.

I approach a class in clowning or magic as a type of performance. As I develop a class, I create a 9 1/2 x 12 1/2 envelope for that class. In that envelope are the notes for the class, the original copies of handouts I intend to use, and any visual aids I develop specifically for that class. There is also a list of all the props and other visual aids that class requires. When I am scheduled to teach that class, I pull out its envelope. I use the visual aid list as I pack for the class. If I am teaching more than one class at a conference or convention, I pack a book bag with the props for each class. If there are things I will need for an earlier class or performance, I put a Post It note on the envelope to remind me that class is not complete. Then just before the class, I double-check my list to make sure that I have everything.

During December, I perform a Christmas variety show as Santa Claus. The props for that show all go into a box that is stored in the attic with our Christmas decorations. Inside that box is a script for the show, and a list of additional props I need from other shows I perform during the year. When it comes time to do that show, it is easy to get things out and ready.

My most complex performance is my *Tramp Tradition Show*. It has a wide variety of routines, and includes some simple costume changes. For that show, I not only have a packing list, but a list detailing where each prop needs to be at the beginning of the show. I list what needs to be in each pocket of my costume, in the coats I put on during the show, on an off stage table, in my trunk on stage, and on my magic table on stage. Without that list, I could never remember where things need to be. Also, I often have a limited time at conventions to prepare for that show, and following the list lets me quickly put things where they belong. Looking over the list reassures me that everything is prepared so I can relax and concentrate on what I will be doing during the performance itself.

Not only do I need to have my props organized, but I also need to have my thoughts organized before the show. I don't do my best performance if I rush in at the last moment and have to begin. I start getting my props set long before it is necessary. I determine how much time I think I need to drive to a location, and then add an extra half-hour to allow for traffic or getting lost. Then if I reach the location early, I find an inconspicuous place to park and allow myself a little quiet time to get my thoughts in order.

For some of my performances, routines need to go in a specific order for things to work out. For example, in my Sorcerer's Apprentice act, I produce a silk during one routine and then use that silk in a later routine. If I forget to produce it, I can't do the second routine. For those shows, I list the routines I will be doing in their order, and put the list someplace where I can easily see it, but the audience can't. During the show, if I can't remember what comes next, all I have to do is glance at the list.

There is a method of organization that works best for each person. Carole is most comfortable with props in labeled cardboard boxes. They are organized and they look neat. For me, out of sight is out of mind. I like to be able to see things. My props go on shelves or into plastic drawers with clear fronts. Things look cluttered, but I can locate things at a glance.

What can you do before a performance to insure it is successful? What method of organization works best for you?

# Ask for Assistance

You do not have to know how to do everything. You just have to know how to find the people who have the necessary knowledge and skills.

The story of R. U. Darby was told by Napoleon Hill in *Think and Grow Rich*. Darby discovered gold in Colorado. The vein appeared to be a large one, but unexpectedly it ran out. The miners did exploratory digging searching for the continuation of the vein, but couldn't find it. In frustration, Darby sold the land to a junkyard dealer. The new owner called in a mining engineer. The engineer was trained in geology and knew how rock formations often shifted. He surveyed the land, and calculated where the vein should resume. They dug in that location, and discovered he was right. The vein was located just three feet from where Darby had stopped digging.

The little plastic cannon that I was refurbishing had two large plastic wheels. A third of one of the wheels had broken off. I did not know how to fix the wheel. I asked my father, who was an industrial arts instructor. He made two wooden wheels on the lathe that were perfect for that prop.

When Lou Jacobs was working on his little car, he did not know how to get it to run. He asked George Wallenda, mechanical expert of the Wallenda wire-walking act, for help. According to Fred Bradna, George adapted a washing machine motor to power the car.

Ralph Huntzinger wanted to build a magic effect described in an old book. While the operation of the effect was described, the dimensions weren't given. The effect used wooden blocks. Ralph asked me to help with deciding on a size. I got out as many square objects as I could find, and we played around with them. We decided some were too big to handle easily. Others were too small to be seen by the audience. Gradually, we narrowed the possibilities down until we agreed on the best possible size. Ralph constructed the effect, and used it very successfully in his shows.

When Carole needs to have something done, she begins networking. She asks her friends if they know somebody who has had something similar done. Eventually, she finds somebody who knows somebody who knows the information she needs.

What additional knowledge do you need to complete your project? Who do you know who has that knowledge? If you don't know anyone yourself, how can you spread the word that you are looking for that information?

## Solutions To Similar Problems

You do not have to start from scratch with every project. Other people may have found effective solutions to similar problems and you can adapt what they have done. Thomas Edison said, "Make it a habit to keep on the lookout for novel and interesting ideas that others have used successfully. Your idea has to be original only in its adaptation to the problem you are working on."

To make a print requires applying pressure to transfer ink from the block or type to the paper. Originally the process was very time consuming because it was done by rubbing the back of the paper with a spoon by hand. Guttenberg wanted to speed up the process which required developing a way to apply uniform pressure to the entire surface of the paper at one time. While working on the problem he took time off to attend a wine festival. There he saw a wine press that was used to apply uniform pressure to squeeze all the juice out of a bunch of grapes. He realized that was the solution to his problem. He bought a wine press and turned it into the first printing press.

What is similar to what you want to do? How have others accomplished that? How has it been done in the past? How can you adapt what they did to what you want to do?

## Utilize Technology

Modern technology can help in the design process. For example, whenever I need to make a sign, I first lay it out using my computer. With just a few clicks of the mouse, I can try different lettering styles and sizes. I can change the proportions. I can rapidly try alternate versions until I decide on one that I think is the most pleasing. Then I print it out. Depending upon the size of sign I am making, I use the print out to make a stencil or use an opaque projector to enlarge the design.

Computers can also help speed up the construction process of paper items. Early in my career, I would sometimes perform a personalized magic effect. For example, I would show both sides of a blank piece of paper, tear it up, and drop the pieces into a Drawstring Change bag. I would add a felt pen, close the bag, and give it a shake. Then I would reach into the bag's other compartment to remove a duplicate felt pen and a whole piece of paper with a message appropriate to the event, for example, "Welcome to the XXX Company Picnic." I would carefully hand letter the message as neatly as possible. Often it took me an hour to complete it. Using a computer, I can create and print the message in a few minutes. Since the computer makes it so easy to create a personalized message to be produced by magic, I do that in almost every show I perform.

When I made my first customized version of the *Magic Coloring Book*, it was an alphabet book. I did all twenty-six drawings by hand, and then took them to a print shop to have them transferred to card stock. That particular book had only black and white drawings. The first time I made one that was colored, I pasted and glued the colored pages after the black and white ones were printed. After getting a computer, I discovered that I could use computer clip art files to make customized magic coloring books and print the graphics directly on the card stock. I could print out both black and white and colored versions of the same image. I could now do in a day what originally took me weeks to do.

In addition to helping with planning, modern technology can help you make something physically happen. Arthur C. Clarke said, "Any technology that is sufficiently advanced will seem like magic."

Here are some ways that entertainers have used modern technology.

The early puppet shows on TV were done as if it was a live performance and the camera substituted for the audience. Part of the reason the Muppets became so successful is that Jim Henson explored the possibilities of his new medium and took advantage of the technology. He used different lenses and camera movements to create the illusion that his puppets had a wider range of movement. He used blue screen technology to incorporate simple illusions and special effects into his puppet performances. Technically, the Muppets were hand puppets, but Jim Henson and his creative crew did not use a purist approach. To achieve some of the effects they wanted, they incorporated mechanical and electronic devices into the construction of the puppets.

Some magicians now use technology similar to Disney's AudioAnimatronics to create moving body parts for illusions. For example, the Thin Model Sawing In Two originally used mannequin legs to make it appear the assistant's legs were separate from her body. Animating the false legs so they move realistically greatly enhances the illusion.

Sean Bogunia uses computer chips to program things like a dancing handkerchief routine. Once you have programmed the prop, you simply have to push the start button and the movements are automatically repeated for each performance. He uses radio controls for some of his other motorized effects.

Some entertainers use radio-controlled cars to power a motorized prop. In *The Magic of Thinking Creatively*, Barry Mitchell describes how to use a radio-controlled car to build a remote controlled card fountain. I have also seen props that suddenly come to life because they are built on top of a radio-controlled car. I do an old clown gag where I drop my hat, and when I move forward to pick it up, I kick it out of my reach. For a brief time in the 1980s, I did a version that used a duplicate hat on a radio-controlled car. Just as I got close to the hat, it would start to move. I stopped using the routine because it was not appropriate for the venues I was working in.

The Flying Karamozov Brothers juggling team worked in collaboration with the Massachusetts Institute of Technology in creating their stage show *Luniverse*. Some of the routines relied on sonar to keep track of the position of the performers on stage. In one routine, moving their arm cued a computer to produce a musical note. The note produced depended upon the position of the performer on stage. When they moved, the note changed.

In another routine in *Luniverse*, the Flying Karamozov Brothers formed a marching band. They marched around the stage, and then behind a large screen at the back of the stage. As they disappeared behind the screen, a video began which showed the band upon the screen. The entertainers switched their instruments for juggling props and marched out the other side of the screen. They then juggled to their own musical accompaniment that they had previously videotaped. The routine was scripted so that the live entertainers interacted with their video selves.

At one time, close up magic was limited to intimate settings because the props could not be easily seen in large theaters. Many magicians have successfully performed close up magic on stage by using video cameras hooked up to video projection systems to project close up shots of what is happening on large screens.

I have used a video projection system for doing trick cartoons for an audience of five hundred people in a theater.

I have experimented with using Microsoft's PowerPoint program to incorporate graphics into my shows. I have used it to produce act title signs like they used in vaudeville. When I have worked for large audiences, I have used it to project the words on signs that I normally use in my show, making sure everyone could read the text. In gospel ministry presentations, I have used it to project the text of Bible verses that I am using in routines. I have also used it with doing trick cartoons. To insure that the screen matches what I draw, I print out the slide, and then use a pencil to lightly draw the picture on my newsprint pad. The audience can't see those lines during my performance, but all I have to do is trace over the lines with a marker to make the finished drawing match what will appear on the screen. To the audience, it appears that the screen is copying me.

At the 2002 Clown Ministry Impact Conference, a group of clowns performed a silent movie style routine. They used PowerPoint to do the dialogue signs.

Kenny Ahern has said, "Use technology, but don't trust it. Always have backups."

I was in a variety show where two magicians were using radio signals to remotely trigger an effect. (They were both card tricks.) Both effects did not work at the matinee. The magicians had to apologize to the audience for not being able to conclude their act successfully. The magicians tested the effects after the show, and they worked without problem. During the evening show, the effects did not work again. We experimented after the show. We discovered that both magicians used the same wireless microphone during their act, and the frequency it was on apparently jammed the signal for the trick. After that performance, one of the magicians made sure he always had a second way to reveal the selected card. He tries the radio-controlled effect first because that gets the best audience response. If that does not work, he uses the second revelation to provide a finish to the act.

One of the effects they were using has a reputation for unreliability. The manufacturer even advertises, "Where would the challenge be if it worked every time?" It uses a motor to pull a cotter pin out releasing the gimmick. If I were using that effect, I would attach a second line to the cotter pin so it could be pulled manually.

When you see a new invention or hear about a new product, ask yourself, how can that be adapted for use in my show? When working on a project, ask what method is possible that did not exist before? Then when you find a new solution, ask what back up can I use in case this technology fails?

## Audience Perceptions

In addition to figuring out how to make something happen physically, you have to figure out how to make it happen psychologically.

Mike Caveney said, "The best magic never happens except in the minds of the audience." What actually happens is unimportant compared to what the audience perceives happened. For example, if the audience did not realize you had put a coin into your left hand, they will not be amazed when you open your hand revealing that the coin is gone. However, if they think you put a coin in that hand, even if you don't have any coins, they will be amazed to discover that the hand is empty.

Magicians talk about misdirection, which is actually a poor term for what happens. That implies that you are directing their attention away from something that you don't want them to see. Having somebody shoot a blank pistol at the back of the room when you are ready to do a difficult sleight will make the audience look away so they do not see what you are doing. That is misdirection. However, that is not magic, because there is no sense of wonder. They think they know how the trick was done even if they don't know the exact mechanics. They know something devious was done while they were so obviously distracted. A good magician directs the audience's attention to what is important for them to see. The theatrical term "focus" is a better way to think about it. You use color, timing, contrast, movement and stillness, pointing, and other tools to make sure the audience is looking where they are supposed to look at the right time.

Comedy also happens only in the mind of the audience. A simple description of a joke is that you cause the audience to think one thing and then surprise them by making them suddenly think of something else. Often you start them thinking about one definition of a word and then change to a different definition. Remember the cow joke that switched from the definition of "Long" from duration to size. The set up for a joke is how you make them think what you want them to. Timing is allowing people to think what you want without anticipating the switch. If you rush the cow joke too fast, they don't think about duration so there is no surprise when you talk about size. If you go too slow, they guess the punch line so there is no surprise. When a joke does not get the response you want, the problem usually is not with the punch line but with the set up. The solution is to look at the start of the joke and figure out how you can strengthen the mental image the audience has before the punch line.

Audience perception is important in making juggling entertaining. Entertainers who juggle large numbers of objects need to emphasize what they are doing. To a lay person, anything over four is perceived as just being a lot. Although I am a juggler, I sometimes have trouble counting more than five objects in a pattern. If a juggler does seven rings, they need to find a way to count them out so the audience understands what is happening. Also, some juggling tricks happen so quickly that the audience does not get to see what happened. One solution is to explain in advance what you are attempting to do. Another solution is to repeat a trick several times so the audience knows what to watch for.

Visibility is an important key to perception. The audience has to see it to understand it.

Color and contrast play an important role in visibility. I saw a magician perform a Chinese Linking Ring routine with beautiful brass rings. They created a richer look that the aluminum rings normally used. However, from the back of the audience I had trouble seeing what he was doing. He performed most of his moves in front of his body and the rings visually blended into his gold brocade vest. The rings and vest were similar in color. The pattern of the vest formed a camouflage design that made it even more difficult to distinguish the shape of the rings. If he had worn a solid black or blue vest, the rings would have been easy to see.

All performers need to be aware of their background. Props held in front of the body need to be a contrasting color to the costume. I tend to use blue for my costume and backdrops, and most of my props are either red or yellow. I originally wore a black hat with my tramp costume. I noticed in photos of my stage performances that the hat tended to blend in with the black curtains. Since my hat is an important prop for me, I switched to a gray hat that is easier to see.

Angles are important for visibility. Magicians often talk about angles in terms of hiding something, but they are even more important in displaying what is important. For example, many magicians display a deck of cards by fanning them out horizontally near their waist. This may put the cards below the sight line of everyone seated beyond the second row. Those who can see the cards get a better view of the edge of the deck instead of the faces. More people could see the faces of the cards if the magician were to raise their hands, and fan the cards out vertically at chin level with the faces towards the audience. Not only would the audience be able to see the cards easier, but they could also see the cards and the performer's expression at the same time. If the cards are fanned, the audience just gets to see a small portion of each card. If you really want them to perceive that the cards are all different, display them individually by moving them from the deck to the other hand. This allows the audience to see the entire face, but also creates the subtle impression that you are changing the order of the cards so the way they are stacked is unimportant.

Angles are important for a juggler as well. Some tricks are easier to see from the side than from the front. Rings should usually be juggled so the audience sees them from the side instead of the edge. That means the juggler should stand facing the audience with the rings perpendicular to their arms or the juggler should stand with their side to the audience. When doing tricks with clubs, you should experiment to see what angle makes it easier for the audience to see what is happening.

In creating perceptions, it is often more effective to be subtle. If you say a Change Bag is empty, you raise the audience's suspicions. They wonder why you said that. It is more effective to pull scarves out of the bag one at a time, and then grab the bottom of the bag and pull it inside out as if you thought there was another scarf there. The audience can see for themselves that the bag is empty and they think they understand why you turned it inside out.

One of the most effective ways to convince the audience that something is normal is to handle it as if it was normal. I saw a magician performing for a group of his peers take a deck of cards out while still talking about his previous trick. He did a couple of overhand shuffles as if he was fidgeting. When he finished his comments, he handed the deck to somebody in the front row to shuffle. While they were doing that, he made some introductory remarks to the card trick. Since he did not pay any attention to the deck being shuffled, nobody else did either. He retrieved the deck, and then did a card trick that amazed everyone. Afterwards, he revealed that all fifty-two cards in the deck were duplicates. Since he had casually let somebody else handle the deck, everybody had assumed it was a normal deck. We did not suspect he would be brave enough to let somebody handle a gimmicked deck. The person who shuffled the cards had no reason to suspect that the cards were not normal so they did not inspect them. They concentrated on the order of the cards instead of the appearance of the cards.

When turning an idea into something to perform you need to ask four questions. What do I want the audience to think? What is the best way to make them think that? What is important for the audience to see? How can I make that more visible?

## Performance Aids

Once I figure out how to make an idea work, I take it a step further and figure out how to make it work smoothly. For example, if I have to unfold a piece of paper during a performance, I fold it so the edges do not meet. That makes it easy to grasp the edge without fumbling during performance.

I spend as much time figuring out where to place a prop so I can pick it up smoothly as I do figuring out how to use it.

Sometimes a packet card trick requires that the cards be turned a specific way. (For example, one of the cards may have a half card on back that is concealed during the first part of the trick.) When I set up one of those tricks, I make the face of the top card an odd numbered club, heart, or spade. I think of the pips as arrows. I know that the cards are oriented in the correct direction if the majority of the pips are pointed at the audience.

When you turn your idea into reality, ask what will make this easier for me to perform? What will prevent accidents from happening? What can I do so I don't have to think more than necessary about the mechanics?

## Simplify

Most people have heard of KISS—Keep It Simple Stupid. Magician Tommy Wonder says that is wrong. That implies that what you start with is simple and all you have to do is keep it that way. I know that most of my ideas start off being too complicated. I have to work hard at simplifying. To me it is like chipping away the rock to find a diamond, and then cutting even more to give it the desired shape. Tommy Wonder suggests that a better anagram would be MISS—Make It Simple Stupid.

Many clowns initially make their make-up design too complicated. For example, they may paint rainbows on their cheeks and over their eyebrows. In effect, the extra designs form a camouflage pattern on their face making it harder for the audience to see their expressions. A simpler design makes their face more expressive. Clowns often use a hodge podge of colors for their wardrobe thinking that makes them look bright and colorful. However, a lot of small areas of color blend together visually and can begin to turn to grey. In my college costume classes I learned that to make a costume seem bright you use large areas of one color bordered by small areas of the contrasting color. When I critique clown appearance, I spend a lot of time encouraging people to simplify.

I was reminded of the power of a simple routine when I was employed as a magician to do in store promotions for International Home Foods. Their advertising campaign was titled Cook Up A Little Magic With Your Kids. My job was to perform magic and distribute coupons. Each coupon had a silver square. Scratching the square with a coin revealed a discount offer that varied on each coupon. I decided to use a small Drawstring Change Bag to distribute the coupons. I cut a matching piece of blank paper. I had the kids put the blank paper into the bag. I had them wave a magic can of Pam over the bag. (Pam is one of the IHF products.) Then I let the kids look inside the bag to discover that the paper had turned into a coupon. I was surprised by their response. They expressed more amazement at that transformation than they did at my more elaborate sleight of hand routines that I had spent a long time developing. I think the appeal of this routine was that they got to do the magic themselves, it was easy to understand what happened, and the result was something that they got to keep. Then I would produce a coin from behind their ear and let them use that to scratch the coupon. That also got a great response. Finally, when they were done, I made the coin disappear.

My ideas for magic routines often start off too complicated because I try to prove things that don't need to be proven. For example, an appearing cane is a spring coil that is collapsed and held in place with a lever. There is an eyelet at the end of the lever.

Frequently the magician attaches something to the eyelet. When the lever is released the coil expands covering up what is attached. The first time I did a Rope To Appearing Cane effect, I sewed the eyelet on the collapsed cane about three inches from the end of the rope. I thought that way I could let the end of the rope extend out below my hand to show that nothing was attached to the rope. There was plenty of room within the cane to hide a double thickness of rope. However, that meant when the cane expanded it had to fold the rope in half before it could cover it. That slowed the transformation just enough that it didn't look right. I realized that I didn't need that. Ropes usually do not have something attached so people would not suspect that there is something there. I reattached the eyelet to the end of the rope and the simpler set up worked much smoother. As far as I know, nobody has ever seen me pick up a piece of rope and thought, "I wonder if he has an appearing cane attached to it." Audience response has proven that they are completely surprised by the transformation.

Simplifying a routine makes it easier to understand. A magician performing in a circus had three large boxes in the ring and a cage suspended above the ring. He had one assistant in the cage, and two more assistants got into boxes. Simultaneously, the cage and three boxes fell open. I think the first assistant had vanished from the cage and reappeared in the box the second assistant had gotten into, the second assistant was in the box the third assistant had gotten into, and the third assistant was in the box that had previously been empty. I asked somebody who had accompanied me to the performance what they thought had happened. They weren't sure. All they could remember was that a bunch of people got into boxes and a lot of people got out of boxes.

Master clown Lou Jacobs would tell students at the Ringling Bros and Barnum & Bailey Clown College™ to "cut the spaghetti." He meant cut out anything that was unnecessary. Everything in a clown routine should get a laugh, evoke some other emotion, reveal character, or move the plot along.

Lou Jacobs

Ernie Bushmiller, creator of the "Nancy" comic strip, said, "I leave out all extraneous detail that may detract from the main point. I try to get some black into the object I am stressing if it is at all feasible. In a visual gag strip, clarity is more important than artistic effect. Composition is extremely important. By composition, I mean intelligent placing of your objects and characters so as to make it as easy as possible for your reader to get what you're driving at."

A concept in magic is simplicity of effect and simplicity of method. Simplicity of effect means that an audience member can explain what happened in one sentence. Simplicity of method means that the easiest possible method is used to produce the desired effect. When you use the easiest method, less can go wrong.

In one card trick, after the card is selected you have somebody play an audiocassette in a tape player and a voice announces the chosen card. The first person that I saw do this was Nick Weber performing with his Royal Lichtenstein Circus in 1983. He used a method to force a card that matched the message on the pre-recorded tape. Over fifteen years later, I saw another magician teach his version of the effect. The way that magician had the card chosen seemed unnatural to me, and later he explained that his method forced one of four possible cards. He had to find out the identity of the selected card before he put the tape in the player because the revelation for two of the cards was on side A and the revelation for the other two cards was on side B. If the first card on the side was chosen, the tape had to be shut off right away before any more of the tape was heard. If the second card was chosen, the tape was allowed to run. There was a joke about the first card not being the selected one and then the other card was named. I don't know what the advantage was of having four possible cards chosen. To me it made things more complicated and added more things that could go wrong. You could put the cassette in the wrong direction so the wrong cards were revealed. Since the tape had to be able to play in both directions the recorded segment could not be at the beginning, which made cueing the tape more difficult and increased the chances that it might be cued wrong. Also, it left your routine to chance. Half the time it would be amazing, and half the time it would include some humor, and you would have no control over what it would be for a specific show. Simplifying the trick means that you could use an easy method that would force only one card. That is what Nick had done. Then you would make only one recorded message that could be at the beginning of the tape where it is easy to cue it up and double check to see that it was ready. If you decided the joke was really that effective, you would include it in every performance. Simplifying the routine also increases the mystery value because you would not have to touch the tape player after the name of the card was announced. Another advantage was that you did not have to find out the identity of the chosen card before it is revealed.

Some people think using a simple method means using props that do not require any skill. It seems that clowns in particular are drawn to these effects described as "self-working." However, the simplest way to do something may be using sleight of hand. Some of the self-working props make the effect more complicated. For example, instead of picking up a coin and making it vanish, you have to pick up the coin, place it in some type of container, close the container, open the container, and then prove that it is empty.

A method requiring skill can be easy. A magician complimented me on how well I did a difficult move in one of my routines. At first, I did not understand what he meant because to me the move is easy. Then I realized that the reason it is easy for me is that I have done it so many times. It also seems easy because it is well within my skill level and I do other moves that I consider more difficult. It is easy only by comparison.

Simple routines must still be done well. Dr. Harlan Tarbell, in *The Tarbell Course in Magic Volume One*, wrote, "You will find many of the tricks very simple in method, yet in spite of their simplicity, you cannot do them well until you have mastered the principles and the moves and the fundamentals and can present them in a finished manner. Many of the details of magic are so simple that you might be tempted to make the mistake of thinking them unimportant. That mistake is fatal. When explained, these details are ridiculously simple. Yet, how mystifying to your audience."

The easiest solutions often take the longest to find. One reason it is so hard to simplify things is that you invest so much time and effort in your ideas. It is easy to fall in love with them making it difficult to let them go.

Another reason it is hard to find simple solutions is that you get used to doing something and don't think about an easier way to do it. You assume that the way you have been doing it is the way it should be done. In one of my routines I produce several scarves with pictures of clowns on them. I use a prop called a Phantom Tube to do that. A Phantom Tube has two walls. The outer wall is straight. The inner wall is tapered. Silk scarves can be hidden in the space between the walls. If you look through the tube from the end where the walls are joined, an optical illusion makes it seem that you are looking through an empty tube with a thin wall. If you look through the other end of the tube, you will see the scarves in their hiding place.

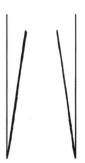

Phantom Tube Cross Section

I use a Phantom Tube to produce one 36-inch scarf and several 18-inch scarves. The large scarf and one of the smaller ones have a dark blue background. The large scarf fills one half of the tube. The other scarves go in the other side. The first scarf to be produced goes in last so when you look in the top of the prop you see its background color. For a long time I produced the eighteen-inch scarf with the dark blue background first. That meant I could not tell just by looking into the prop which side had the large scarf and which side had the small ones. I tried different ways of secretly marking the side that I wanted to start with. Then I finally realized that I did not have to produce that scarf first. I changed the order of the scarves so the first one has a yellow background. Now it is very easy to tell at a glance which side to use first.

Another aspect of simplification involves your personal life. If your life is so busy and hectic that you don't have the time or energy to realize ideas you can't be very creative. You often have to simplify your life before you can be creative.

One of my costume teachers in college knew that she would have a lot of decisions to make the last two weeks before a production premiered and that she would be required to spend many hours in the costume shop. So, during those two weeks she wore a uniform. Everyday she wore blue jeans and the same sweatshirt that she had chosen that related in some way to the production. That way she did not have to decide what to wear each day. During the run of the show, she wore casual clothes because she was at the shop late. Then when the show was over, she indulged her personal fashion sense and would often be fashionably dressed.

When I am working on finishing up a new prop or routine, especially with an approaching deadline, I will make a large casserole that leaves enough leftovers for dinner several days. I don't have to decide what to eat, and I don't have to take time to prepare it. I simply have to put a serving on a plate and heat it.

What can you do to simplify your life? What is most important to you? What is something that you can eliminate to give you more time and energy for those things that are important?

## Additional Quotations

*"Anything that looks graceful and effortless and easy usually has a lot of grueling work behind it."—Peggy Flemming*

*"I learn by trial and error, not by trial and accuracy. Our greatest glory is not in never failing, but in rising every time we fail."—Thomas Carlisle*

*"Creativity is a habit, and the best creativity is the result of good work habits."—Twyla Tharp*

*"The simplest explanation is usually correct."—Occam's Razor*

*"Action will remove the doubt that theory cannot solve."—Tehyi Hsieh*

*"If you don't take a few chances, you might as well stay in bed."—M.C. Escher*

*"Dreams come true; without that possibility, nature would not incite us to have them."—John Updike*

*"What would life be if we had no courage to attempt anything?"—Vincent van Gogh*

*"I'm a great believer in luck, and I find the harder I work, the more I have of it."—Thomas Jefferson*

*"Knowledge is of no value unless you put it into practice."—Anton Chekhov*

*"Genius is ninety-nine percent perspiration and one percent inspiration."—Thomas Edison*

*"A solution should be as simple as possible, but no simpler."—Einstein*

*"Opportunity is missed by most people because it is dressed in overalls and looks like work."—Thomas A. Edison*

*"Far better it is to dare mighty things, to win glorious triumphs, even though checkered by failure, than to take rank with those poor spirits who neither enjoy much or suffer much, because they live in the gray twilight that knows not victory nor defeat."—Teddy Roosevelt*

*"I can accept failure. Everyone fails at something. But I can't accept not trying."*—Michael Jordan

*"Success is not permanent, neither is failure."*—Unknown

*"If you doubt you can accomplish something, then you can't accomplish it. You have to have confidence in your ability, and then be tough enough to follow through."*—Rosalyn Carter

*"It's not enough to be creative if you can't execute. It's not enough to execute if all you are building is something that people don't want."*—Lance Nokumiru, Verifone

*"Ideas without action is like being all dressed up with no place to go."*—Harvey Mackay

*"When you are trying a new bit of business, put it between two safe bits, so if it fails, you can quickly recover."*—Arthur Pedlar

*"When you try a new bit, and it doesn't work, it is hard to know if it is a bad idea or the timing was off or you didn't sell it correctly. Never base a decision on just one try. Try performing it four or five times, altering it a little, and you may discover that it suddenly works right."*—Arthur Pedlar

*"My father believed there were no shortcuts to be had in the life of the dedicated artist. There is only faith and persistence."*—Monte Schulz, son of Charles Schulz

*"Simple is not simplicity. Simple is elegant."*—Unknown

# Going Fishing

We will use writing patter for a magic routine to give you practice in using this four step process of creativity. The routine uses a deck of Go Fish cards so we will be writing fish jokes. Although I am using the jokes for a magic trick here, the same process works for other types of routines. A juggler can tell fish jokes while juggling with fish shaped beanbags or clubs. A puppeteer might use the jokes with a fish puppet. What fish props might work in your act? How could you use some of the fish jokes that you will write with those props?

## The Genesis of the Routine

When I worked at Raging Waters, they requested that I perform as many water related routines as possible. I bought a commercially available magic trick called Sammy Seal. In this effect, a balloon is attached to the nose of a cut out seal. A card is selected and returned to the deck. (You force the card.) Then the balloon bursts and the card chosen card is balanced on the seal's nose. Normally this trick is done with a deck of poker cards. Any type of deck can be used. To fit my theme, I used a deck of Go Fish Cards. The routine I came up with worked very well in stage shows. However, it can't be done surrounded because seeing the back of the seal will reveal how the trick works.

I did many atmosphere shows at the park where the audience surrounded me. One of the things I had been doing was a Linking Rope routine. The basic effect is excellent, and the method is clever. Magnets in the ends of two pieces of rope allow you to open and close a loop of rope. I have seen people do wonderful linking rope routines. However, I was dissatisfied with the response that I was getting to the routine I had created. I decided to replace it with a trick using fish cards that I could do surrounded.

At a magic shop, I saw a demonstration of a trick where the selected card was lassoed. I realized that the trick worked with magnets in the rope. A short piece of rope was tied around a duplicate of the card that would be chosen. The free end of the rope had a magnet inside. A long piece of rope also had a magnet in one end. When the end of the rope was lowered into a container, the magnets came into contact. Withdrawing the rope revealed the card tied on the end. I realized that I could use the rope with magnets from my linking rope set to create a similar routine. Only in my version I would go fishing and catch the selected card. In my routine, you have a volunteer pick a card from a Go Fish deck. You try to find the card but fail. Finally you drop the deck into a bag, and lower in one end of a rope into the bag. When you lift the rope out of the bag, the bottom has bent into a fish hook shape and the chosen card is impaled on it.

## Being an Explorer

The first step is to list as many words as you can that are associated with fish. In your explorer role, try to find as many words as you can, using all the resources available to you. The more words you come up with now, the more fun you will have when you switch to the artist role. Here are some questions to help you in your search.

> What are the parts of a fish?
> What are the different kinds of fish?
> Where do you find fish?

What else do you find in their environment?
What can you do with fish?
What do fishermen have or use?
What stories about fish do you know?
What songs include fish in their title or lyrics?
When you eat fish, what else is on the menu?
What resources do you have available to add to
   your answers?

Here is a short list that I will use as an example for the following steps. How many more words can you add to it?

Scale, Fin, Gill, Porpoise, Cod, Shark, Bass, Gold, Flounder, Tuna, Aquarium, Shoal, Ocean, Sushi, Hook, Sinker, Mermaid, Cole Slaw, Chips

# Being an Artist

When you have as many fish words on your list as possible, it is time to shift into the artist role. Now you will play with the words and create new associations. Remember to delay shifting into the judge role. Your goal is to create as many potential jokes as possible. Don't worry about whether they are good or not. At this point all ideas are valid. A joke you ultimately decide is poor may turn out to be the inspiration for a better joke.

### Words with Multiple Definitions

Look for words that have more then one meaning. For example, scale means: 1. Overlapping covering on a fish. 2. A type of insect. 3. Oxide coating forming on heated iron. 4. Removing the scales from something. 5. To throw a thin flat object. 6. To climb to the top. 7. Any system of designating measurement units, e.g. Fahrenheit scale. 8. A fixed proportion for determining measurements in a model or drawing 9. Musical notes in an octave 10. To rise in steps or stages 11.

A balance. 12. A device for measuring weight. 13. A decision e.g. the scales of justice

Now try to write a line that starts with one meaning of a word and switches to another meaning. For example, "Do you know why fish have scales? It's so they can weigh anchors."

"Do you know why fish are good musicians? They know their scales."

What other lines using more then one meaning of scale can you write?

What other words in your list have more then one meaning? What lines can you write switching from one meaning to another of those words?

### Similar Sounding Words

Try to find words that sound similar to words on your list. For example, "tuna" sounds similar to "tune a." Write a line where you substitute a similar word for one in the original phrase. For example, "Do you know you can tune a piano, but you can't tuna fish?"

Play around with creating variations on an idea. A common clown gag is to put a harmonica into a toy fish so you can demonstrate how to tune a fish.

## Names

Look for words in your list that sound like a name. For example, "sushi" sounds similar to the name "Susie." What phrases and titles do you know with "susie" in them?

A song lyric says, "if you knew Susie, like I knew Susie, oh, oh, oh, what a girl." Again, look for other sound a likes. "Girl" is similar to "gill." That leads us to "If you knew sushi, like I knew sushi, oh, oh, oh, what a gill."

"Mermaid" sounds similar to "merman." Ethel Merman was a famous singer and actress. What was she known for?

Among other things, she was famous for singing "God Bless America" and "There's No Business Like Show Business." Now look at those song titles for words that sound similar to things on your fish word list. "God" sounds like "cod." "Bless" sounds like "bass." "Show" sounds like "shoal." With that information, you can write, "Do you remember Ethel Mermaid's big hits? Cod Bass America and There's No Business Like Shoal Business."

# Being a Judge

When you have created as many jokes as possible, change to the role of judge and evaluate them. Remember to stay positive. Look for jokes you like or portions of jokes that you like. For example, in the Ethel Mermaid joke I like "There's No Business Like Shoal Business." I mark that for use. If I had been focused on looking for jokes to eliminate, the Cod Bass America pun might have made me reject the entire joke and I would miss out on a line that I have used successfully for many years.

Which jokes do you like? Here is a system that works for many people. Place a check mark next to them. Set the list aside for a little while. Then read the jokes you checked, and circle the check mark of those that you really like.

# Being a Warrior

When you have a list of possible jokes for a routine, it is time to switch to the warrior role and turn the routine into a reality. (By purchasing this book, you receive the rights to make this routine for your own use. However, I am retaining all manufacturing rights to this and all the other routines in this publication.)

First, you will need to decide how you are going to force the selected card. Select a method that you know or turn to volume 3 and pick one of the ones described there. If you are going to use a sleight of hand method to do the force, you will need only one deck. However, if you are going to make a gimmicked forcing deck you will need to determine how many decks of cards you need to purchase to get enough duplicates. Perhaps at this point you will discover you don't like any of the methods that you know, and will return to the Explorer role to read magic books looking for other options. Purchase the Fish cards you need from a toy store.

Next, prepare the rope. The easiest way to do it is to buy a set of Linking Ropes. The short piece is just the right length. You could also start with magician's rope, remove part of the core, and insert your own magnets.

Using a standard hole punch, make a hole in one card near the character's mouth. Thread the short piece of rope through the hole. Bend the rope in half, and sew the two halves together at their midsection. (Halfway between the card and the magnet.) Bend down the side without the magnet to form the hook's barb. Sew it together near the bend to maintain its shape.

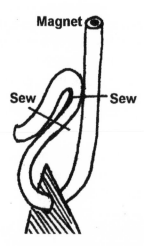

Next, decide on the container that you will put the cards into. I like to use a Drawstring Change Bag for this routine. That allows me to keep the gimmicked rope and card separate from the deck making it easier to make the magnetic connection and pull the card out. I've also performed it in the past using a paper bag. Using a bag works well for me because I perform this in walk-a-round and atmosphere settings. Other containers are possible. For example, you could make a fish bowl with the duplicate card and short piece of rope in a compartment hidden in the sand. What kind of container would work best for you? How would you hide the gimmick?

Now take your favorite jokes and put them together in an order that makes sense to you. Look at the individual jokes to see if they can be improved. Is there some way you can make the set up stronger for each joke? What changes will make the punch line for each joke easier to understand?

The next step is to practice the routine until you feel comfortable with it. Then perform it in front of an actual audience.

## Working and Presentation:

Here is one possible presentation of the routine.

With the deck toward the audience, peel some cards off one at a time so they can see what type of deck it is and aren't surprised when a fish is chosen.

You can incorporate some of your fish jokes while doing this. For example, if your deck has a card depicting a shark, explain that it is a card shark.

"Do you know why fish have scales? . . . So they can weigh anchors."

"You can tune a piano, but you can't tuna fish."

"Do you remember Ethel Mermaid's big hit, 'There's No Business Like Shoal Business?"

Start singing, "If you knew Sushi like I knew Sushi, oh, oh, oh what a gill."

Use your favorite method to force the choice of the card you want chosen. Have the volunteer return the card to the deck. You can either hold the deck in your hand while you look for the card, or drop it into the bag and try to find their card by touch. Pull out wrong cards a couple of times. It has been said, "A wise entertainer lets his audience feel superior at times without letting themselves become inferior." Making these mistakes allows your audience to feel smart, but you are going to regain their respect by succeeding in a manner they can't explain.

Depending on your performance style and character, you can add fish puns about your difficulty. For example, the first time you are wrong, comment, "I did that on porpoise to make it look harder," or, "you enjoy seeing me flounder, don't you?"

Announce that you are going fishing since the trick didn't work right. (If you are still holding the deck, drop it into the bag.) Lower the magnetic end of the long piece of rope into the bag. Make sure that the end you are holding stays in sight the entire time. Let the two magnets click together. Announce that you think you got a bite. Shake the rope as you pull it out of the bag so that it looks like there might be something wiggling on the end. (Besides being good presentation, this has a practical purpose. The ends of the rope don't always align perfectly. The shaking will cause the magnets to shift into complete contact.) Draw the rope out revealing that you have caught the selected card, and acknowledge your applause.

For a juggler using these jokes while juggling fish props, the Warrior step would be different. You will need to decide what type of props you will use. Will you juggle Goldfish crackers, beanbags shaped like fish, clubs that look like fish, or another prop? If you are going to use clubs that look like fish how will you construct them? Will you purchase rubber fish at a novelty store and stiffen them? Will you decorate actual juggling clubs so that they look like fish? What materials will you use? Would you decorate a pool cue stick so it looks like a sword fish and use it for balancing routines or as a stick for a spinning plate routine? Once you decide upon the props, you would need to gather the necessary materials and build them. Then you would write your routine and practice it.

If you perform another variety art specialty, what would the warrior step be like for you? How would you incorporate fish jokes into what you do? What would you need to do to prepare the routine for performance?

## Return to the Judge

Now you are going to return to the role of judge, and let the audience join you. What parts of the routine were awkward to perform? What did the audience laugh at? What did they respond to in other ways? What did they not respond to? What are the strongest parts of the routine? How can they be reinforced? What were the weakest parts? Can they be strengthened or do they need to be removed? Do you need to put something else in their place or is the shorter version better?

## Tangents

Be willing to follow tangents while going through this process. While I was working on Going Fishing, I created another card trick for use on stage. A Visual Painting is a type of magic effect where you begin with a black and white drawing and magically it becomes colored. When I listed places where you find a fish, I wrote gold fish bowl. It wasn't practical for me to use a real fish bowl at Raging Waters, but I could use a picture of a bowl. That led me to making my own customized Visual Painting that began with a black and white picture of a cat standing on top of an empty bowl. I had a volunteer select a card and then paint in the picture. When the picture became colored, a picture of the selected fish appeared in the bowl. For a short period, at clown and variety arts conferences I sold some of the props for this routine that I had hand painted. David Ginn purchased one and can be seen performing it on his *Bag of Magic* video tape.

I am not going to describe how the trick worked here. There are many ways to turn a black and white picture into a colored one. If I describe just one, you might assume that is how it has to be done. If you like the idea, become an Explorer and find ways to accomplish the effect. Then Judge the best one and turn it into reality. Your solution may be better for you than mine.

# Hot Dog

Now we will practice the process using a different type of routine. It will be a Visual Pun where you use objects to present an alternate meaning of words.

In the 1970s, I began seeing a product called an Invisible Dog Leash at toy stores and joke shops. It is a stiff leash with a harness that makes it appear you are walking a dog, but there is nothing there. I knew some clowns who used an Invisible Dog Leash in parades. However, my theory is that people won't laugh at anything they may have purchased themselves. The theme of the 1980 Carson & Barnes Circus Spec was The Clown Is King. Everyone in the show's cast would be in a clown costume for this parade around the Hippodrome track. The show's producers asked me to create some extra parade props that others could use during the Spec. I knew that a traditional clown gag was to carry a hot dog, a live dog in a giant prop hot dog bun. I decided to reverse that and use the Invisible Dog Leash to take a hot dog for a walk. I had not seen anybody do that before, but have seen it many times since then.

We will start with creating the prop, and then write a routine for it. Often I discover more ideas while playing with a prop.

## Explorer

This may seem silly, but the first step is to fix a real hot dog. If you are going to make a prop hot dog, you have to know what a real one looks like. Don't assume that you know. Get a hot dog and look at it. You can stylize it and leave out some details, but first you need to know what it is really like. This may lead to some additional ideas. For example, preparing your hot dog may remind you that you like to eat your hot dog with ketchup on it.

## Artist

I have already played artist for you and made the connection between a hot dog and a pet.

## Judge

Consider your ideas about the appearance of your hot dog. For example, do you want to make your prop look like it has ketchup on it? What is the advantage of doing that?

## Warrior

Now you will decide how to make your hot dog and then actually construct it. My original hot dog was a tube of red fabric stuffed with fiberfill and gathered at the ends. It looked like a hot dog, but was a little heavy. I used pieces of foam rubber to make the two halves of the bun and attached everything together with contact cement.

When I attended Clown Camp® in 1986, Mark Anthony taught a class on foam prop carving. Mark taught me how to use an electric kitchen carving knife to carve foam. Under his guidance, I carved a new hot dog and bun out of a single piece of foam rubber.

There are several potential ways to color the foam rubber. A method Mark taught me was to mist the foam with water from a spray bottle, and then draw on the foam with pastel chalk. The water draws the pigment down into the foam. You finish by spraying the foam again lightly to settle any residual chalk dust.

Another method to color foam rubber is to spray paint the foam using Floral Spray (AKA Designer Colors) available from craft stores. This spray was created by florists to color white flowers—like chrysanthemums—for arrangements.

A third method is to give the foam a coating of latex to create a smooth texture. Paint will not adhere to the latex. So, the last coat of latex should be mixed with an equal amount of acrylic paint. When this is dry, acrylic paint will adhere to it and you can paint on details.

I have not experimented with it, but I know that many puppeteers use fabric dye to color foam. I understand that you need to test the dyes first because they react differently with the foam than they do with fabric and may produce an unexpected color.

Do you know of another method that might work better? Which method would you use?

Most clowns use an oversized foam rubber hot dog for this prop. That is not the only possibility. I saw it done one time with a normal size plastic hot dog and bun purchased from a toy store. Then it was obvious that the harness was too big for the dog. However, the harness could be taken in to make it look right. What materials would you use for your hot dog?

If you have decided on putting condiments on your hot dog, what would they be made out of? How would you attach them?

While creativity is often described as a four-step process, you don't always do it in only four steps. Now that you have the prop, it is time to return to the Explorer mode and create the routine that will go with it.

## Explorer

Start playing around with the hot dog in the leash. Have fun with it. What happens if you twirl the leash between your fingers? Can you make the hot dog sit up? Ask yourself what happens if? . . .

I am going to explain a little different method of organizing your ideas that may inspire some additional ideas.

Start by making two columns. At the top of the first column, write "food." At the top of the second column, write "animal."

In the first column, write down everything that you can think of that you associate with the type of hot dogs that you eat. Think about types of hot dogs, things you put on hot dogs, things you have along with hot dogs, places you find hot dogs, songs about hot dogs, and anything else you associate with hot dogs.

In the second column, write down everything you associate with dogs as animals. Think about types of dogs, parts of their body, things dogs do, where you see dogs, names of dogs, people you associate with dogs, songs about dogs, and anything else you can think of.

You don't have to complete one list before you start the next. Switch back and forth as new ideas occur to you. When you run out of ideas, experiment with incubation. Take a break and do something else. Engage in some type of physical activity. When you come back, see if any more ideas have come to mind.

Again, for demonstration purposes I am giving you a short list. How many words can you add to each column?

| Food | Animal |
|---|---|
| Buns | Pure Bred |
| Ketchup | Papers |
| Mustard | Police Dog |
| All Beef | Tail |
| Ballpark Frank | Buns |
| Bread | Leash |
| Napkin | Collar |
| Sausage | Bark |

## Artist

Once you have as many words as possible on both lists, start comparing them looking for things in common. For example, hot dogs come in buns, and buns are a part of a dog's anatomy. When you find those, try to write a line that utilizes both meanings. A possibility is "I know he looks kind of funny, but doesn't he have nice buns?"

Things don't have to be an exact match, for example, napkin and papers. Is there some way you can switch from one to another? Perhaps you will say, "He's pure bred. Would you like to see his papers?" Then you would pull out a napkin to display.

What things do you find in common on both of your lists? What comedy lines can you write using them?

Once you have considered all the things the lists have in common, work with each list separately. Again, look for words with more then one meaning. For example, mustard is a condiment. "Cutting the mustard" means passing the requirements for a job. If we select the second meaning as our punch line, we then need to decide on the job he would attempt. Perhaps we would use "police dog" from the animal list. That would give us the line, "He wanted to be a police dog, but he couldn't cut the mustard."

Look for variations of lines. Perhaps Ballpark Frank makes you think of baseball. That would give us, "He loves baseball. In fact, he wanted to be a ballpark frank, but he couldn't cut the mustard." What things do you associate with baseball? One that comes to my mind is people saying, "Let's see a little pepper out there?" An alternate line could be "he loves baseball. In fact, he wanted to be a ballpark frank, but he couldn't stand the pepper."

What words do you find on your lists that have more than one meaning? What comedy lines can you write using them?

Next, look for words that sound like others. For example, "sausage" sounds similar to "saw such." A possible line is "I bet you never sausage a dog before."

## Judge

Now look at all the potential lines and bits of business that you have written. Decide which ones you like best.

## Warrior

Take the lines and bits of business that you like and put them into a logical order. Is there any way you can change some of the lines to make them stronger? Often I start out with too many words and have to edit things down.

Next, actually perform your routine.

## Return to Judge

Pay attention to audience reaction. After your performance, ask yourself, what could be done to improve the things people responded to positively? What similar ideas can I add? What things need to be eliminated or replaced?

## Other Variations

The hot dog idea does not have to be used as a clown parade routine. A puppeteer might make a hot dog puppet and treat it as a pet. A comedy magician may announce that they are going to make a dog appear and then produce a hot dog in a bun. A clown could enter with a portable dog crate, announce they are going to make a dog vanish, pull a hot dog out of the crate and eat it. I've seen balloon sculpture hot dogs. One of these could be given a balloon leash and taken for a walk? How could you use the hot dog idea?

You could use the Invisible Dog Leash to take other types of animals for a walk. I once saw a clown with a toy car in a leash. He lifted the car off the ground and swung it through the air. Then he announced that it was his Flying Car-Pet. What kind of pet would you have? How would you construct the props? What jokes could you use while performing with it?

# The Creative Process Review

## Multiple Guess

Can you guess the answer to each of these questions?

1.  Making something become true by acting as if it is true because you believe it is true is
    A. Serendipity    B. Synchronicity
    C. Serengeti      D. Self-fulfilling Prophecy

2.  Turning your idea into reality is called
    A. Serendipity    B. Synchronicity
    C. Incubation     D. Implementation

3.  During the artist phase it is important to delay
    A. Gratification  B. Payment
    C. Judgment       D. Beginning

4.  Trying to come up with as many potential ideas as possible is
    A. Convergent Thinking    B. Divergent Thinking
    C. Confused Thinking      D. Distracted Thinking

5.  Graham Wallas was the first person to describe creativity as a four-step process. His fourth step was
    A. Implementation    B. Illumination
    C. Incubation        D. Intuition

6.  According to Randy Pryor, "Before you can be good you
    have to be . . .
    A. Smart          B. Lucky
    C. Bad            D. Rich

7.  Finding what you are looking for is called
    A. Serendipity    B. Synchronicity
    C. Serengeti      D. Self-fulfilling Prophecy

8.  Taking time off from a project to allow your subconscious
    to play with it is
    A. Implementation      B. Illumination
    C. Incubation          D. Intuition

9.  Imitation is
    A. Flattery       B. Limitation
    C. Creation       D. A Shortcut to Success

10. Roger von Oech described four roles in the creative
    process. Which two are mutually exclusive?
    A. Explorer       B. Artist
    C. Judge          D. Warrior

11. Left Mode thinking is like
    A. Reading a book       B. Looking at a painting
    C. Riding a bike        D. Riding a roller coaster

12. Right Mode thinking is like
    A. Reading a book       B. Looking at a painting
    C. Riding a bike        D. Riding a roller coaster

13. Just being different is not enough, to be creative an idea
    must be
    A. An Improvement       B. Copyrighted
    C. Sold                 D. A Commodity

14. Making a fortunate discovery while looking for something else is

    A. Serendipity   B. Synchronicity

    C. Serengeti    D. Self-fulfilling Prophecy

15. Narrowing possible ideas down to the one you will use is

    A. Convergent Thinking  B. Divergent Thinking

    C. Confused Thinking    D. Distracted Thinking

16. Knowing the answer without being sure of the reason is

    A. Implementation     B. Illumination

    C. Incubation        D. Intuition

17. The most important step in the creative process is

    A. Serendipity   B. Synchronicity

    C. Incubation     D. Implementation

18. To succeed you have to be willing to risk

    A. Failure      B. Fame

    C. Your Fortune D. Your Life

19. According to Scott Hamilton, integrity and perseverance

    A. Pays off     B. Makes you a sucker

    C. Is uncreative D. Is boring

20. To be creative an idea must be

    A. Obscene    B. Unique

    C. Appropriate  D. Stolen

21. During the Judge role you should start out by looking for

    A. Flaws      B. Lawyers

    C. Strengths   D. Profit Margins

22. According to John Welsh what percentage of your ideas will tend to be good ones?

    A. 10 percent   B. 20 percent

    C. 50 percent   D. 90 percent

23. Which of the following does not need to be appropriate for ideas you use in performance?
    A. Diet        B. Audience
    C. Time       D. Material

24. According to Eugene Burger, the best reason to be creative is
    A. A marketing tool      B. Being different from others
    C. Becoming famous      D. Being true to yourself

# Are You in Your Right Mind

Identify the following characteristics as being associated with Right Mode Thought or Left Mode Thought

1. Verbal
2. Visual
3. Random
4. Logical
5. Conscious
6. Subconscious
7. Music
8. Mathematics
9. Movement
10. Linear
11. Drawing
12. Memories
13. Analytical
14. Decisive
15. Generates New Ideas
16. Evaluates Existing Ideas
17. Intuitive

# Answers

## Multiple Guess

1.D., 2.D., 3.C., 4.B., 5.A., 6.C., 7.B., 8.C., 9.B., 10. B. & C., 11. A., 12.B., 13.A., 14.A., 15.A., 16.D., 17.D., 18.A., 19.A., 20.C., 21.C., 22.A., 23. A., 24. D.

## Are You In Your Right Mind

1. Verbal—Left Mode 2. Visual—Right Mode 3. Random—Right Mode 4. Logical—Left Mode 5. Conscious—Left Mode 6. Subconscious—Right Mode 7. Music—Right Mode 8. Mathematics—Left Mode 9. Movement—Right Mode 10. Linear—Left Mode 11. Drawing—Right Mode 12. Memories—Right Mode 13. Analytical—Left Mode 14. Decisive—Left Mode 15. Generates New Ideas—Right Mode 16. Evaluates Existing Ideas—Left Mode 17. Intuitive—Right Mode

## Nine Dots

This is one possible way to connect the nine dots with four straight lines.

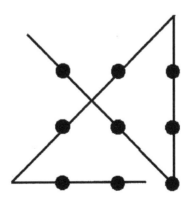

# Glossary

**Artist Role:** Step in creative process where you generate new ideas

**Assessment:** Determining the relative strengths and weaknesses of an idea.

**Beginner's Mind:** Being open to new ideas without preconceived solutions.

**Breakaway:** 1. Prop constructed so that it appears to break when you want 2. Prop constructed to break safely and easily

**Cascade:** The basic juggling pattern where each object traces an infinity sign in the air.

**Conscious:** Part of your mental activities that you are aware of and have come control over

**Convergent Thinking:** A technical term used in many publications on creativity meaning narrowing down many possibilities to the one you will use.

**Dichotomy:** Two opposing concepts kept in balance.

**Divergent Thinking:** A technical term used in many publications on creativity meaning starting with one point of inspiration and generating as many potential ideas as possible.

**Expert Mind:** Having the necessary knowledge to implement an idea

**Explorer Role:** Step in creative process where you search for information or inspiration

**Force:** To apparently give somebody a free choice, but they can only select what you want them to, e.g., method of making them select a card with a specific identity from a deck. A force can be accomplished by sleight of hand, psychological principles, or using specially prepared props.

**Happy Accident:** A random or unintentional occurrence providing a benefit or opportunity.

**Illumination:** Moment of insight when you become aware of an idea

**Immersion:** Learning everything you can about a project and attempting to find a solution in preparation for incubation.

**Implementation:** Turning an idea into a reality.

**Incubate:** Doing something else to give your subconscious a chance to work on your project.

**Intellectual Property:** An idea that is considered the property of the originator. Like other forms of property it has value, can be sold, and should not be stolen by others.

**Intuition:** Reaching a conclusion without being sure of the reasons.

**Judge Role:** Step in the creative process where you evaluate your ideas deciding which ones to implement

**Left-Mode Thought:** One of the two modes of thinking. It is logical, sequential, analytical, and verbal. It is sometimes referred to as your Conscious. Left-Mode Thought controls the right side of your body.

**Plagiarism:** Stealing intellectual property or written material belonging to another

**Public Domain:** Something that is no longer the property of a specific individual or company frequently because of the length of time that has passed since it was originated

**Right Mode Thought:** One of the two modes of thinking. It is random, visual, and spatial. It involves music, movement, and drawing. It is where your memories are stored and where new connections between thoughts are made. It is sometimes referred to as your Subconscious. Right-Mode Thought controls the left side of your body.

**Self-fulfilling Prophecy:** Something that may or may not be true, but because you think it is true, you act as if it is true, which makes it become true.

**Serendipity:** Finding something useful while looking for something else.

**Simultaneous Creativity:** two or more people working independently from each other coming up with the same idea. It is often thought of as occurring at the same time, but it can be somebody recreating an idea without knowledge of the previous version

**Subconscious:** Part of your mental processes that you are not aware of and do not control

**Suspend Disbelief:** 1. In theater, the audience willingly pretends temporarily that what they are seeing is actually happening. 2. Delaying judgment, especially skepticism and doubt, until you have finished generating ideas and it is time for assessment.

**Synchronicity:** Finding something because that is what you are looking for.

**Ten Percent Rule:** An estimate that 10 percent of your ideas will be useable

**Transposition:** A magic effect where an item vanishes from one location and reappears in another location.

**Warrior Role:** Step in creative process where you make your idea a reality

# Bibliography
# and Suggested Reading

## Books

Adams, Scott *The Joy Of Work: Dilbert's Guide To Finding Happiness At The Expense Of Your Co-Workers* New York: Harper Business, 1998

Aleinikov, Andrei G. *MegaCreativity: 5 steps to Thinking Like a Genius.* Cinncinnati, OH Walking Stick Press, 2002

Allen, Steve with Wollman, Jane *How To Be Funny: Discovering The Comic You* New York: McGraw Hill, 1987

Allen, Steve *More Funny People* New York: Stein and Day, 1982

Allen, Steve *Steve Allen's Private Joke File* New York: Three Rivers Press, 2000

Anderson, Brad *Top Dog: Marmaduke at 50* New York: Ballantine Books, 2003

Andrews, Bart *The "I Love Lucy" Book* Garden City, New York: Doubleday & Company, Inc., 1985

Ayan, Jordon *Aha! 10 Ways To Free Your Creative Spirit and Find Your Great Ideas.* New York: Three Rivers Press, 1997

Bartlett, David *The Clown Star: Five Points To Guide You Toward Continual Progress* Durham, NC: Understanding Wife Publishing, 2003

Baird, Bill *The Art Of The Puppet* New York: Ridge Press, 1973

Benny, Jack and Joan *Sunday Nights At Seven: The Jack Benny Story* New York: Warner Books, Inc., 1990

Berk, Ronald A. *Humor As An Instructional Defibrillator* Sterling, Virginia: Stylus, 2002

Berle, Milton *Milton Berle's Private Joke File* New York: Crown Trade Paperbacks, 1989

Bishop, George *The World Of Clowns* Los Angeles, Ca: Brooke House Publishers, 1976

Bishop, Leonard *Dare To Be A Great Writer 329 Keys To Powerful Fiction* Cincinnati, OH: Writer's Digest Books 1988

Block. Lawrence *Spider, Spin Me A Web: Lawrence Block on Writing Fiction* Cincinnati, OH: Writer's Digest Books 1988

Blythe, Cheryl and Sackett, Susan *Say Goodnight Gracie! The Story of Burns & Allen* New York: E. P. Dutton, 1986

Brown, Joe E. and Hancock, Ralph *Laughter Is A Wonderful Thing* New York: A.S. Barnes and Company, 1956

Burns, George *Gracie A Love Story* New York: G. P. Putman's Sons, 1988

Cahn, William *Harold Lloyd's World of Comedy* New York: Duell, Sloan and Pearce, 1964

Cahn, William *The Laugh Makers* New York: Bramhall House, 1957

Canemaker, John *Walt Disney's Nine Old Men & The Art of Animation* New York: Disney Editions, 2001

Carlyon, David *Dan Rice: The Most Famous Man You've Never Heard Of* New York: Public Affairs, 2001

Carter, Judy *Stand Up Comedy—The Book* New York: Dell Publishing, 1989

Christopher, Milbourne *The Illustrated History of Magic* New York: Thomas Y. Crowell Company, 1973

Christopher, Milbourne *Magic: A Picture History* New York: Dover Publications Inc., 1962

Clark, Hyla M. *The World's Greatest Magic* New York: Tree Communications Inc., 1976

Connellan, Tom. *Inside The Magic Kingdom: Seven Keys to Disney's Success.* Austin, TX: Bard Publishing, 1997

Conrad, Barnaby and Schulz, Monte *Snoopy's Guide to the Writing Life* Cincinnati, OH: Writer's Digest Books 2002

Cook, John *The Book of Positive Quotations* Minneapolis: Fairview Press, 1993

Cook, Marshall, *Freeing Your Creativity: A Writer's Guide.* Cincinnati, Ohio: Writer's Digest Books, 1992

Crandall, Rick (editor) *Break-Out Creativity: Bringing Creativity to the Workplace* Corte Madera, CA: Select Press, 1998

Dardis, Tom *Keaton: The Man Who Wouldn't Lie Down* New York: Charles Scribner's Sons, 1979

Davis, Jr., Sammy and Boyar, Jane and Burt *Why Me? The Sammy Davis, Jr. Story* New York: Farrar, Straus, and Giroux, 1989

Deschner, Donald. *The Films Of W. C. Fields.* Secaucus, NJ: The Citadel Press. 1966

Dimeglio, John E. *Vaudeville U.S.A.* Bowling Green, OH: Bowling Green University Popular Press, 1973

Downs, T. Nelson *The Art Of Magic* New York: Dover Publications, Inc., 1980

Edwards, Betty *Drawing On The Artist Within: An Inspirational and Practical Guide to Increasing Your Creative Powers* New York: Simon & Schuster, Inc., 1986

Edwards, Betty *The New Drawing on the Right Side of the Brain: A Course in Enhancing Creativity and Artistic Confidence* New York: Jeremy P Tarcher/Putnam, 1999

Faith, William Robert *Bob Hope: A Life In Comedy* New York: G. P. Putnam's Sons, 1982

Fein, Irving A. *Jack Benny: An Intimate Biography* New York: G. P. Putnam's Sons, 1976

Feynman, Michelle *The Art of Richard P. Feynman: Images by a Curious Character* Amsterdam BV: The Gordon & Breach Publishing Group—Overseas Publishers Association, 1995

Feynman, Richard *"What Do You Care What Other People Think?" Further Adventures Of A Curious Character* New York: Bantam Books, 1988

Feynman, Richard *The Pleasure Of Finding Things Out* Cambridge, Massachusetts: Perseus Books, 1999

Fields, W.C. *Fields For President* New York: Dodd, Mead & Company 1939

Fields, W.C. *W. C. Fields By Himself* New York: Warner Books, Inc., 1973

Finch, Christopher *Jim Henson The Works—The Art, the Magic, the Imagination* New York: Random House, 1993

Finch, Christopher *Of Muppets & Men: The Making of the Muppet Show* New York: Muppet Press/Alfred A. Knopf, 1981

Fischbacher, Siegfried and Horn, Roy *Siegfried and Roy: Mastering The Impossible* New York: W. Morrow, 1992

Fitzkee, Dariel *Showmanship For Magicians* Oakland, CA: Magic Limited, 1945

Flemming, Peggy *The Long Program: Skating Towards Life's Victories* New York: Pocket Books, 1999

Frank, Leonard Roy *Quotationary* New York: Random House, 2001

Franklin, Joe *Joe Franklin's Encyclopedia of Comedians* Secaucus, NJ : The Citadel Press, 1979

Frewin, Greg *Creativity: Putting Your Visions To Work* Self Published Lecture Notes, 2003

Fry, William F. and Allen, Melanie *Life Studies of Comedy Writers* New Brunswick (U.S.A.): Transaction Publishers, 1998

Gelb, Michael *How To Think Like Leonardo Da Vinci: Seven Steps to Genius Every Day* New York: Delacorte Press, 1998

Gilbert, Douglas *American Vaudeville Its Life and Times* New York: Dover Publications, Inc., 1940

Girsh, Maria and Charlie *Fanning The Creative Spirit.* [S.1.] Creativity Central, 1999

Gorman, Ed and Greenberg, Martin H. *Speaking About Murder* New York: Berkley Prime Crime, 1998

Gribbin, John and Mary *Richard Feynman: A Life In Science.* New York: Dutton, 1997

Guiles, Fred Lawerence *Stan: The Life of Stan Laurel* New York: Stein and Day, 1980

Hamilton, Scott with Benet, Lorenzo *Landing It: My Life On And Off The Ice* New York: Kensington Books, 1999

Hausner, Lee and Schlosberg, Jeremy *Teaching Your Child Creativity.* Washington D.C.: Lifeline Press, 1998

Hay, Henry *The Amateur Magician's Handbook* Third Edition New York: Signet Books, 1972

Helitzer, Melvin *Comedy Techniques For Writers and Performers* Athens, OH: Lawhead Press, 1984

Helitzer, Melvin *Comedy Writing Secrets* Cincinnati, OH: Writer's Digest Books 1987

Howard, Pierce J. Ph.D. *The Owner's Manual For The Brain: Everyday Applications from Mind-Brain Research* Marietta GA: Bard Press, 2000

Imagineers, Walt Disney *Imagineering: A behind the dreams look at making the magic real.* New York: Hyperion, 1996

Jenkins, Ron *Acrobats Of The Soul* New York: Theatre Communications Group Inc., 1988

Johnston, Lynn *A Look Inside For Better of For Worse—The Tenth Anniversary Collection.* Kansas City, Missouri: Universal Press Syndicate, 1989

Johnston, Lynn *It's The Thought That Counts . . . For Better of For Worse Fifteenth Anniversary Collection* Kansas City, Missouri: Andrews and McMeel, 1994

Johnson, Bruce. *Comedy Techniques For Entertainers.* LaCrosse, WI: Visual Magic, 1988

Jones, Chuck, *Chuck Amuck: The Life and Times of an Animated Cartoonist.* New York: Farrar Straus Giroux, 1989

Jones, Chuck *Chuck Reducks: Drawing From The Fun Side Of Life* New York: Warner Books, 1996

Josefsberg, Milt *Comedy Writing For Television & Hollywood.* New York: Harper & Row, 1987

Josefsberg, Milt *The Jack Benny Show: The Life and Times of America's Best-Loved Entertainer* New Rochelle, New York: Arlington House Publishers, 1977

Josephson, Matthew *Edison* New York: McGraw Hill, 1959

Kachuba, John B. *How To Write Funny* Cincinnati, OH : Writer's Digest Books, 2001

Kao, John *Jamming*. New York: Harper Colllins, 1996

Katkov Norman *The Fabulous Fanny: The Story of Fanny Brice* New York: Alfred A. Knopf, 1953

Keaton, Buster & Samuels, Charles *My Wonderful World of Slapstick* New York: Ca Capo Press, 1960

Keeshan, Bob *Good Morning Captain* Minneapolis, Minnesota: Fairview Press, 1996

Keeshan, Bob *Growing Up Happy* New York: Berkley Books, 1989

Kelly, Emmett with Kelley, F. Beverly *Clown: My Life in Tatters and Smiles* New York: Prentice-Hall, Inc, 1954

Kidd, Chip *The Art of Charles Schultz* New York: Pantheon Books, 2001

Kline, Jim *The Complete Films of Buster Keaton* New York: Citadel Press, 1993

Knobf, Robert *The Theater and Cinema of Buster Keaton* Princeton, New Jersey: Princeton University Press, 1999

Kunzog, John C. *The One-Horse Show: The Life and Times of Dan Rice, Circus Jester and Philanthropist* Jamestown, NY: John C. Kunzog, 1962

Laflin, Duane *Greater Gospel Magic* Greensburg, Indiana: Winters Publishing, 2000

Leuzzi, Linda *A Creative Life: The Young Person's Guide*. Danbury, Connecticut: Franklin Watts, 1999

Locher, J.L., editor, *M. C. Escher: His Life and Complete Graphic Work With A Fully Illustrated Catalogue*. New York: Hearry N. Abrams, Inc., 1982

Louvish, Simon *Man On The Flying Trapeze: The Life and Times of W. C. Fields* New York: W. W. Norton & Company, 1997

Lynn, Kenneth S. *The Comic Tradition In America: An Anthology of American Humor* Garden City, NY: Doubleday Anchor Books, 1958

MacGregor, Jerry *Real World Magic*. USA: Jerry MacGregor, 1999

Mackay, Harvey *Pushing The Envelope All The Way To The Top*. New York: Balantine Publishing Group, 1999

Malone, John *The Encyclopedia of Figure Skating* New York: Facts On File Inc., 1998

Maltin, Leonard *The Great Movie Comedians from Charlie Chaplin to Woody Allen* New York: Harmony Books, 1982

Marshall, Brenda *Sharing God's Love Through Laughter: A Guide To Christian Clowning*. North Richland Hills, Texas: Brenda Marshall, 2000

Marx, Arthur *Red Skelton: An Unauthorized Biography* New York: E. P. Dutton, 1979

Marx, Harpo with Barber, Rowland *Harpo Speaks* New York: Limelight Editions, 1961

McCabe, John *Charlie Chaplin* Garden City, New York: Doubleday & Company, Inc., 1978

McCabe, John *Mr. Laurel & Mr. Hardy* New York: Doubleday & Company, Inc., 1961

McCabe, John *The Comedy World of Stan Laurel* Beverly Hills, CA: Moonstone Press, 1990

McDonnell, Patrick *Mutts: The Comic Art of Patrick McDonnel* New York: Harry N. Abrams, Inc. 2003

Meadows, Audrey with Daley, Joe *Love, Alice: My Life As A Honeymooner* New York: Crown Publishers, Inc., 1994

Messer, Mari *Pencil Dancing: New Ways To Free Your Creative Spirit* Cincinnati, Ohio: Walking Stick Press, 2001

Mitchel, Barry *The Magic of Thinking Creatively* Seveirville, TN: Cre8iv Press, 2003

Montanaro, Tony with Montanaro, Karen Hurll *Mime Spoken Here: The Performers Portable Workshop* Gardiner, Maine: Tilbury House Publishers, 1995

Moody, Raymond A. *Laugh After Laugh* Jacksonville, FL: Headwaters Press, 1978

Newton, Douglas *Clowns* London: George G. Harrap & Co. Ltd., 1958

Payne, Robert *Charlie Chaplin (Orig. Title: The Great God Pan)* New York: Ace Books, Inc., 1952

Perkins, David The *Eureka Effect: The Art and Logic of Breakthrough Thinking* New York: W.W. Norton & Company New York, 2000

Perret, Gene *Comedy Writing Workbook* New York: Sterling Publishing Co., Inc., 1990

Peters, Tom *The Pursuit of Wow! Every Person's Guide To Topsy Turvy Times* New York: Vintage Books, 1994

Peters, Tom *The Tom Peters Seminar: Crazy Times Call for Crazy Organizations* New York: Vintage Books, 1994

Reilly, Adam *Harold Lloyd "The King of Daredevil Comedy".* New York, NY: Macmillan Publishing Company, 1977

Ricchiuto, Jack *Collaborative Creativity: Unleashing The Power of Shared Thinking* Akron & New York: Oakhill Press, 1997

Robinson, David *Chaplin: His Life And Art* New York: McGraw-Hill Book Company 1985

Rolfe, Bari Mimes editor *On Miming: Writings On The Art Of Mime* Los Angeles, CA: Panjandrum Books, 1979

Root-Bernstein, Robert and Michele *Sparks Of Genius. The Thirteen Thinking Tools of the World's Most Creative People* Boston, New York: Houghton Mifflin Company, Boston, New York, 1999

Saks, Sol *The Craft of Comedy Writing* Cincinnati, OH: Writer's Digest Books, 1985

Sands, George *3 Sandsational Rope Routines.* Phoenix, AZ: George Sands, 1987

Schulz, Charles M. *You Don't Look 35, Charlie Brown!* New York: Holt, Rinehart and Winston, 1985

Shalit, Gene *Laughing Matters: A Celebration of American Humor* Garden City, NY: Double Day & Company, Inc., 1987

Shallcross, Doris J. *Teaching Creative Behavior: How To Evoke Creativity in Children of All Ages.* Buffalo, NY: Bearly Limited, 1985

Smith, Dave *Disney A to Z: The Official Encyclopedia* New York: Hyperion, 1996

Smith, Eric Ledell *Bert Williams: A Biography of the Pioneer Black Comedian* Jefferson, NC: McFarland & Company, Inc., 1992

Speaight, George *The Book Of Clowns* New York: McMillan Publishing Co. Inc., 1980

Speaight, George *A History Of The Circus*. London: The Tantivy Press 1980

Stein, Charles *American Vaudeville As Seen By Its Contemporaries* New York: Alfred A. Knopf, 1984

Steinbart, Alice *Creating Brilliant Ideas*. Winnipeg, Manitoba, Canada: Gildner-Reynolds 1999

Sutton, Felix *The Book Of Clowns* New York: Grosset & Dunlap, 1953

Swortzell, Lowell *Here Come The Clowns* New York: The Viking Press, 1978

Tarbell, Harlan *The Tarbell Course In Magic Volume 1* New York: Tannen Magic, Inc., 1927

Thomas, Marlo *The Right Words At the Right Time* New York: Atria Books, 2002

Thompson, Charles "Chic" *What A Great Idea: Key Steps Creative People Take* New York: Haeper Perennial, 1992

Tollin, Anthony *Smithsonian Legendary Performers The Best Of Old Time Radio Starring Burns And Allen* Cedar Knolls, NJ: Radio Spirits, 2002

Torvill, Jayne and Dean, Christopher *Torvil & Dean: The Autobiography of Ice Dancing's Greatest Stars* New York: Carol Pub. Group, 1996

Towsen, John H. *Clowns*. New York, N: Hawthorn Books 1976

Treadwell, Bill *50 Years of American Comedy* New York: Exposition Press, 1951

Von Oech, Roger *A Kick In The Seat Of The Pants: Using Your Explorer, Artist, Judge & Warrior To Be More Creative* New York: Harper & Row, 1986

Von Oech, Roger *A Whack On The Side Of The Head: How You Can Be More Creative Third Edition* New York: Warner Books, Inc., 1998

Vorhaus, John *The Comic Toolbox: How To Be Funny Even If You're Not* Beverly Hills, CA: Silman-James Press, 1994

Vox, Valentine *I Can See Your Lips Moving: The History and Art of Ventriloquism* North Hollywood, CA: Plato Publishing, 1993

Walker, Brian *The Best of Ernie Bushmiller's Nancy*, Wilton, Connecticut: Comicans Books, 1988

Waters, T.A. *The Encyclopedia of Magic and Magicians* New York: Facts On File Publications 1988

Shiting, Percy H. *How To Speak And Write With Humor* New York: McGraw-Hill Book Company, Inc. 1959

Wilde, Larry *The Great Comedians Talk About Comedy* New York: The Citadel Press, 1968

Wilner, Barry *Stars On Ice: An Intimate Look At Skating's Greatest Tour* Kansas City: Andrews McMeel Publishing, 1998

Wolfe, Patricia *Brain Matters: Translating Research Into Classroom Practice* Alexandria, VA: Association for Supervision and Curriculum Development, 2001

Wonder, Tommy & Minch, Stephen *The Books of Wonder Volume 1 & 2.* Seattle, WA: Hermetic Press, Inc., 1996

Wood, Monica *The Pocket Muse* Cincinnati, OH: Writer's Digest Books, 2002

Wujec, Tom *Five Star Mind: Games & Puzzles To Stimulate Your Creativity & Imagination* New York: Double Day, 1995

Ziglar, Zig *See You At The Top* Gretna: Pelican Publishing Company, 1982

# Magazine Articles

Christensen, Randy "Engage The Emotions", *Clowning Around*, Aug./Sept. 2001

De Lung, Rick "Playclown Interview: Famous Clown Artist Jim Howle" *Playclown Magazeen* December 1990

Johnson, Bruce "How Effective Are Those Teeth?" *New Calliope* March/April 2001

Laflin, Duane "Are Those Teeth Funny?—Editors Comments" *Happy Magic* May 2001

Maltin, Leonard "The Secrets of Monsters, Inc." *Disney Magazine* Winter 2001-2002

Walker, Lou Ann "Why They Still Love Lamb Chop" *Parade Magazine* April 24, 1994


*Clowning Around* is published by the World Clown Association

*Happy Magic* is published by Laflin Magic, Troy, Montana

*The Juggler's Bulletin* was published by Montandon Magic Tulsa, OK

*New Calliope* is published by Clowns Of America, International

*Playclown Magazeen* was published by Rick De Lung Anaheim, CA

## Videos

Lewis, Shari *Kooky Classics* New York: Family Home Entertainment, 1984

Wonder, Tommy *Visions of Wonder Volume 1-3* L & L Publishing 2003

Wright, Tim *Tim Wright's Multiplying Balls* Tim Wright Productions 2000 trademark requires permission of International Bible Society.

Ringling Brothers and Barnum & Bailey Circus ™, RBB&B™, and *Ringling Brothers and Barnum & Bailey Clown College*™ are registered trademarks of Kenneth Feld Productions.

Clown Camp® is a registered trademark of Richard Snowberg.

# Index

## A

## B

Ingram Content Group UK Ltd.
Milton Keynes UK
UKHW011957100323
418410UK00013B/297/J